NO SUCH THING AS THE TOP

A Father-Son Expedition

by JOHN D. CUMMING

with KRISTIE HENDERSON

GLASS**SPIDER**PUBLISHING

For my family.

Contents

Foreword

This project started as a brief remembrance of my father, Ian Cumming. It was an exercise (or maybe an exorcism) in coming to terms with my grief, analyzing what he meant to me as a father, mentor, and human being, and summarizing what I had learned from my dad over the years. But it has grown and morphed into something quite different from where it began. This book is about Ian's life, but it is also about my life and Ian's influence on my life. It is a multi-generational story of business principles, personal values, and family bonding in the mountains. This is a memoir, and as such, reflects my recollections through the prism of my lens. The dialogue has been recreated from my memory (sometimes with the assistance of friends and family), and some of the events have been compressed to be more concise. I created this manuscript with love and respect for my father; I never intended to offend, and I hope no one takes offense.

My father was an extremely private person, but he wasn't a recluse. When he retired, Leucadia, the company he and his partner Joe Steinberg built from nothing, was valued at many billions of dollars. He was eulogized in a few publications, and the Reagan family, who owned the electric billboards in the Salt Lake Valley of Utah, paid tribute to

Ian on all of the billboards along the highway around the city. The Utah Nature Conservancy, where he was heavily involved for over ten years, published a beautiful book in his memory. Joe Steinberg created a 400-page book detailing the rise of Leucadia Corporation. The scope of what Ian accomplished professionally and philanthropically is truly staggering by any measure—something that a well-articulated search on chat GPT (or whatever the next search technology is) could provide. But not many people knew Ian as I did. My dad was an enigma—he was a steadfast capitalist and a liberal Democrat. He was empathetic yet pragmatic, he was overweight but also light on his feet, he wore custom three-piece suits—and he swore like a sailor, he had a brilliant mind but could be as impetuous as a child, and he was a tough businessman and a caring father. His close friend Mike Zimmerman once said of Dad, "Knowing Ian is like having a group of intense friends, all in one person." Ultimately, he was a complicated, flawed individual, which allowed him to understand and work with all types of people.

Dad was also a natural-born entrepreneur, a neurosis he passed down to me. While Ian never wanted me to "follow him into his crazy world," as he put it, he had the intellectual plasticity and confidence to allow me to explore entrepreneurship and find success on my terms. He also instilled in me a love of nature and the outdoors, which has fueled my life's work. The mountains have been a constant throughout our lives, offering inspiration, challenge, solace, and finally, a resting place. Through nature and nurture, Dad ingrained in me a strong sense of self-reliance, resilience, perseverance, and grace that helped me to forge my path. Ian had extraordinary gifts but many shortcomings, and sometimes, he flat-out drove me crazy. I had no illusions that I could ever be his equal, a goal he never encouraged nor one that I embraced. Ian was the catalyst for the rise of our family, with his standards and work ethic, and I'm proud to be his son. But I am also proud to be me. Ian will always be the man for whom I have the most respect and admiration in this world, and to this day, when someone says I remind them of my dad, it immediately brings tears to my eyes because I have such reverence for him. Ultimately, this narrative is about father-son relationships, the challenges and successes we both experienced throughout our lives and what I have learned during our journey.

Ian grew up in Vancouver, British Columbia, where the First Nations mythology of the Northwest Coast, specifically the Cowichan tribe, is heavily intertwined in the fabric of the community. My grandmother shared stories of the mythical creatures with Ian and his brother when they were boys, and later, she relayed them to me and my brother, David. On several occasions, Dad brought us to one of the local art galleries or the Museum of Anthropology in Vancouver, where we learned about tribal symbolism, and sometimes, we were lucky enough to pick out a trinket for ourselves. I recently visited one of our favorite galleries, and they still remembered my father, though he had not been there in many years.

In Cowichan mythology, various characters are associated with different traits and myths: orca, bear, eagle, thunderbird, octopus, and even mosquito. The Cowichan tribes developed allegories that are informed by their beliefs. As the stories were passed down and adapted throughout the years, no single account was considered "true" or "exact." As I reflected more on Ian's life and legacy, I recalled the myth of the Raven and how much it embodies his multi-dimensional spirit.

The legend goes something like this. When the whole world was completely dark, there was a famous chief with a bentwood box containing the light of the universe, which he hid and protected from everyone. The Raven, who had white feathers at the time, became obsessed with the box and wanted to have it for his use. He devised a plan to transform himself to slip inside the chief's tent unseen and steal the box. It took a bit of trickery and some time to obtain the box, but after he did so, he shape-shifted back into a Raven and escaped through the chimney, where his feathers turned black from the soot. In his hurry to transport his prize to safety, he dropped the bentwood box, and one large shard and several smaller ones fell, becoming the moon and the stars in the sky. He gripped the final ball of light, but an eagle, reveling in his newly lit visibility, began chasing the Raven, who threw the ball into the clouds, and it became the sun. The Raven brought light to the people and, in doing so, transformed the world.

The oral history of the Cowichans depicts the Raven as having two sides. He is creative, intelligent, and adventurous but can also be self-serving, mischievous, and even gluttonous. He is a cunning schemer, always looking for an angle, but also frivolous. He is shadow, and he is light. He can symbolize creation, transformation, knowledge, the complexity of nature, and the delicacy of truth. Another Raven myth depicts the bird stealing salmon and depositing them along the banks of the river to provide food for the people[1]. In my eyes, my father transformed my family's world and the world around him through his contributions to business, philanthropy, and his community. But like the Raven, he was also flawed, playful, reckless, and sometimes maddening. Storytelling has allowed our species to persist and thrive for thousands of years; tales evolve and provide a symbolic prism from which we interpret the world. I certainly hope that some of these stories (especially the humorous ones) will be passed down through generations.

---

[1] *The Raven Steals the Light* by Bill Reid & Robert Bringhurst

The Grand Disappointment

As I looked down at the state of Wyoming, 12,000 feet below me, with only a harness keeping me from certain death, my legs shook like a sewing machine. My palms were covered in sweat even though the rest of my body was frozen. The wind blew right through my Obermeyer sweater into my soul, where my heart was brimming over with fear. I didn't know whether it was the terror or the cold that was making me shake, or both. It was like I'd lost control of my own body. I'd never felt "exposure." I'd never felt nothing but air beneath my feet. Altitude and cold were things I had experienced in the mountains while skiing, but the combination of vertical relief under my feet, cold sharp rocks, and biting winds overwhelmed me, and I couldn't stop trembling.

I was eleven years old and trying to summit Grand Teton—the largest, steepest part of Grand Teton National Park.

Some people in this world don't react to peril. They seem impervious to the self-protective instinct that overwhelmed me on my attempt at the Grand Teton in northwestern Wyoming. Regardless of one's perspective on acceptable risk, at eleven years of age, I was incapable of reasoning through my situation in such a way that I could get control of my emotions. As a result, our team turned around when we were within sight of the summit of the Grand Teton. The frustration I experienced on that day drove me in ways that I wasn't aware of until I was much older, but I'll never forget the feelings of regret, anger, and disappointment I confronted during that adventure with my father.

Here's how this extraordinary situation came about.

Our family had moved to Salt Lake City (SLC), Utah, in the early 1970s, and my dad became friendly with Ted Wilson, who was running for mayor of SLC as a Democrat at the time. Dad was immediately enamored with Wilson's adventurous spirit and the audacity it took to run for a major office in Utah as a Democrat! Ted was a former Exum guide, the guide service that had been guiding the Grand Teton for more than fifty years. Ted was a lovely, kind man, and he was also a badass.

One day my father said to him, "You gotta take us up the Grand!"

The summit of the Grand Teton registers at 13,775 feet, the three-day climbing route involves 3,000 feet of vertical climbing and is recommended for people aged fifteen and older.

Neither one of us had ever climbed up or repelled down a mountain, and I was barely eleven years old, but in Ian's usual way, these issues didn't register as obstacles. If Ted had any misgivings about my age or ability, I never heard them. If my father thought I could do it, then certainly I could and I would. (Dad may have even convinced Ted that I had more skills than I actually did). My dad was often away on business, so the times when we could do things together and I could make him proud were few and far between. I was an eager partner in his escapades, no matter how preposterous. For a brilliant man, sometimes his optimism bordered on naïveté and caused him to make spectacular errors in judgment. But, like the Raven, even his missteps made fantastic stories.

Ted started our training by taking us to Pete's Rock, a top roping place located along Wasatch Boulevard in SLC. It has some pretty good exposure but is not super technical. Neither Dad nor I knew anything about climbing or had ever been roped up, but Dad's hyperactive enthusiasm drove us both. I was an athletic kid, had a decent power-to-weight ratio, and had the driving force desire to earn the respect of my father. After several days of climbing at Pete's Rock, I began to feel more confident, and the trip was planned for early fall of 1978. Dad went to Wolf's Sporting Goods and got some packs, boots, and headlamps. He spent a lot of time buying food; we had pounds of GORP, peanut butter and jelly, and other accouterments for the climb. What he didn't buy were warm clothes or sleeping bags. "Hell, we are skiers, we can just wear ski clothes!" he said.

The walk into base camp at the Grand is notably long and frigid, and I had never hiked with a pack on my back. Worry started to plant itself in my brain, and an ache developed in the back of my throat; this was nothing like I had pictured. Dad and I were both wearing our Obermeyer sweaters, some long johns, and a windbreaker. Dad was sporting knee-high wool socks and a pair of corduroy knickers he had bought somewhere in Switzerland, and I was wearing jeans. As we put up our tent with frozen fingers, I glanced down at my supermarket sleeping bag, and my worry transformed into something darker. We were both underdressed and underprepared for this adventure.

I woke at 1:00 a.m. to the sounds of stoves being set up to cook breakfast. I put on every layer of clothing I brought, already shivering from the cold and my nerves. As I became more experienced at climbing later in life, I realized how nice it would have been to have a big down jacket to hide inside. We started our ascent in the wee hours that morning—me, my dad, and one of his friends—with Ted Wilson guiding us along. We climbed for several hours, and with every step we took, I became increasingly overwhelmed with my physical pain and emotions. This rock that we were climbing was frigid, sharp, dark, and unforgiving. My mind was running an endless loop of dread, fear, pain, and worry about disappointing my dad and his friend. Meanwhile, Dad was his forever-positive self, reassuring me and trying to motivate me to keep going. But his tone implied *stop complaining*. I wept through the whole first pitch of the climb. I cried from pain and anger at my father for not protecting me. He was the center of my world, and he had put me in this vulnerable, unbearable situation. Like the reckless raven, maybe he hadn't fully thought this trip through.

"I'm cold and scared, and I can't do this." I finally declared.

Instead of realizing how far I had come, all I could think about was how horrible I felt and how far we had yet to climb. Ted, in the most loving way, looked at me and said, "I think this is your summit." He then looked at Dad and continued "I'm taking him down."

Ted was empathetic, patient, and kind to me. He set the standard for what I now believe are the greatest traits you can have as a leader. My dad and his friend came with us, and to this day I don't know whether in some way Dad was relieved or annoyed that we didn't summit, but we all descended together.

I thought going up had been hard and scary, but rappelling to descend, leaning back off the mountain was more than I could bear. I can't even remember much of the descent. I only recall getting to the car later that evening and the devastating feeling of failure. My father had faith in me, and I had disappointed him. I was furious at myself, and I was furious at him, but I couldn't escape the fact that I had let us both down. As I reflect on this adventure as an adult, I wonder if my father ever considered that he had failed me by putting me in a situation where I was doomed to fail? Or maybe it was all part of his grand parenting plan? I was scared. I was in pain. But I survived. In the long run, failing probably served me better than summiting.

On the Grand, and at many other times during my life, my father's fervor pushed me in ways that created discomfort (at times verging on agony). It also reinforced my life-long quest to make him proud of me.

The Teton climb was the first lesson in my development of a high pain tolerance—both emotionally and physically. It would take many years, but eventually, I would harness the terror and self-flagellation I experienced on the Grand and turn them into fuel that would allow me to summit Mount Rainier sixty-nine times, as well as reach the summits of Mount McKinley, Aconcagua, Illimani, and many more peaks around the globe. The fear and anger from that day drove me to build one of the largest privately held ski companies in the world. The pain tolerance I acquired would help me to survive two stem cell transplants.

Still, neither of us would ever go back to the Grand Teton.

A Brief History of the Mad Canadian

Ian's Childhood

Ian Cumming was born in Vancouver, Canada, to Elaine Caroll and Fred McNeil in 1940. Fred was in the Air Force, so they only lived together briefly, and the marriage was troubled from the start. By the time Ian was two years old, both parents were already courting their second spouses. The relationship dissolved into divorce, and in 1942 Elaine married John Cumming. They were both highly educated and broadly published—Elaine was a sociologist, and John was a psychiatrist. They were entrenched in the world of academia and had a definite penchant for socialism. In fact, being in business, or "commerce" as they called it, was stigmatized within the family. They presumed that Ian would follow in their footsteps, but he was dyslexic, mischievous, and had an excess of hyperactive energy that didn't fit with their scholarly expectations. Much later in life, he was diagnosed with ADHD. Meanwhile, Dad's half-brother, David, was quiet, thoughtful, and intellectual—like his parents.

While John Cumming did his duty and adopted and raised Ian, Dad often had the sense that he wasn't good enough and described feeling like an alien in his own home, which forced him to develop resilience at a young age. His mother, Elaine (Granny to me), was strikingly smart, bossy, stern, idealistic, critical, and sharp-tongued. Her mother (Granny Granny) was even more so; my father took us to meet our great-grandmother in Vancouver when I was ten years old, and she was in her nineties. My brother David was wearing his Cowichan sweater with the orca, and I was proud to wear the thunderbird. My hair was kind of long (hey—it was the '70s!), and I looked like I had survived a *Lord of the Flies* misadventure. She took one look at me and said, "Who is this scruffy little hippie?" At the time, I thought she was the meanest person I had ever met.

Despite her short stature (5 feet 2 inches), Granny Elaine had a commanding presence and an unmistakable superiority complex. She was difficult but fair. Her deep blue eyes were usually hidden behind spectacles that changed shape from round to oval to square depending on the decade. Her square jawline and strong nose were framed by a short grey bob and severely cut bangs. She came from a generation of women who had to battle for their station in life, and she could aptly be described as a "tough old broad." Her personality served her well in her long, distinguished career as an academic, but perhaps not so well as a mother. If you pronounced something wrong or used a word incorrectly, she was down your throat, sometimes venomously. She was not a warm and fuzzy, fresh-baked cookies type of Granny, and my dad was downright afraid of her.

In our family, we have what we refer to as "Grannyisms." Any time anyone feels like they have better information and can contradict a statement made by someone else in the family, they are goaded into doing so. The objective, according to the family folklore, is to collect as many "granny points" as possible. This is a competitive, one-upmanship type of activity that offers all players the opportunity "to be right" and show up their fellow family members. There were many "chiefs" in our family, trying to talk over each other, and my grandmother would often use her antique Cowichan carved talking stick to organize the group.

Ian's parents had moved to Kansas to teach at the University of Kansas and that is where Ian attended high school. It was there that he met Jay Nichols of the wealthy and powerful J.C. Nichols Family. Jay recalled the first time he met Ian, "My friend Mike Lynch pulled up (he was the social leader of the group) and I looked over to see Lynch taking a piss on my dad's old Plymouth station wagon, and Ian was standing next to him." Jay's parents, Martha (Marty) and Clyde had the kind of house where all of the teenagers congregated. They spent many an evening gathered in the garage listening to modern jazz and discussing British film and sports cars while drinking copious amounts of beer. Ian never liked beer, and he didn't like to smoke weed either; he liked to be in control. One time his friends convinced him to try some cannabis cookies and he got so ravenously hungry that he opened the jar of peanut butter, spread it across his hands, thick to the edge of his fingers, just like a peanut butter and jelly sandwich, and began licking his fingers. The close-knit group called themselves the Bohemian Hobos or the BOHOs for short.

Finding the Right Path (College, Med School, Failed Love)

After graduating from Shawnee Mission High School in Overland Park, Kansas, Ian began his formal secondary education at McMaster University in Ontario. According to family legend, his stint there did not last long because his mischievous Raven side was prominent in college, and he orchestrated an unsanctioned "panty raid" that led to his expulsion. Consequently, he transferred to the University of Kansas (KU) and rented an apartment with his friend and fellow BOHO, Jim Kramer.

Ian's adoptive father, John, gave him $75/month for an allowance to live on. Ian had a car, so he would drive Kramer around. In return, Jim would buy the groceries and do the cooking. Jim was famous for buying cheap cuts of meat, and the nightly dinner menu would often include beef liver. One night Ian couldn't stand it anymore, and he threw the liver out the window, pan and all. His creative solution to obtaining better cuts of meat was to jimmy the window of the Beta house nearby, and the two of them would sneak in and "borrow" steaks from the frat house to supplement their diet.

Conceding that intellectual pursuits were the only form of currency that his mother accepted, Ian majored in zoology as an undergrad. While at KU, he met Jane Robinson, a beautiful, creative cellist, whom he was infatuated with and married after college. Ian's family always believed that he would make a superb surgeon because he was dexterous, self-assured, and quick-thinking. Eager to please his parents, he enrolled in medical school at KU right after graduation. While Ian was trudging through his first year of med school, enjoying physical work with cadavers but hating chemistry, Jane was traveling with the Kansas City Symphony. On more than one occasion she would call Ian and let him know she was going to bed with one musician or another. He begged her to stop, but she didn't—or couldn't. Finally, Jane's father noticed her erratic behavior and took her for a psychiatric evaluation, where she was diagnosed with schizophrenia, which was severely misunderstood in the 1960s and there were few options for treatment. Jane's father had her committed to the psych ward and suggested that Ian cut himself loose from the marriage to save them both.

Birth of a Capitalist

This stressful turn of events left Ian at a crossroads. He was unhappy at medical school, newly divorced, and feeling somewhat lost. The only omnipresent force in his life was his relationship with the Nichols family. Jay had recently returned from graduate school, and Ian was once again ensconced in their lives. They spent a lot of time hanging out and having adventures in the old Greyhound bus that Clyde had converted into a camper and named the *Pawhuska* after an Osage town in Northern Oklahoma. Ian loved driving the *Pawhuska* and took down a portico or two during his adventures with the Nichols gang. Marty and Clyde Nichols were everything that Elaine and John Cumming were not—inclusive, comfortable, and nonjudgmental. It was the type of family situation that Ian had always envisioned, and he genuinely loved the Nichols family. Often while the rest of the young college students were in the garage, Ian would be in the library talking with Jay's parents. Clyde was warm and humorous, but not very adept at evaluating people or businesses. Marty, on the other hand, recognized talent and quickly became a big fan of Ian; she found him highly intelligent and engaging.

The Nichols were prosperous and lived a luxurious lifestyle—made possible by their involvement in "commerce." Ian was aware of wealth from his days at Fessenden, a boarding school in West Newton, Massachusetts, that he had attended while John and Elaine were traveling professors at Harvard University. At Fessenden, Ian had witnessed private limousines picking up his classmates, but he had never truly tasted affluence until his time with the Nichols family in high school and college. It was during these formative years that Ian's capitalist dreams were ignited. Jay recalled, "I brought Ian into my family and both my parents loved that I did that. I never had one second of regret. They both fell in love with Ian." Marty in particular sensed that there was something special about Ian, and she prompted Clyde to mentor him, which he was happy to do. At Clyde's urging, Ian decided to officially drop out of medical school and work for the Nichols family. Clyde had made a hasty investment in a toy company that didn't work out, so he offered Ian a job liquidating the inventory of toys, which were stored in the salt caverns underneath Kansas City. He must have done a good job because Clyde then offered him a subsequent position with one of their more successful companies, Turner Uni-Drive, at the gear train and transmissions facility.

Dad quickly worked his way up to Foreman at Turner Uni-Drive, which he was tremendously proud of.

♫ *"The working class can kiss my ass cause I've got the foreman's job at last!"*♫ he would merrily sing, in his best Broadway imitation, tone-deaf voice.

While working at the small manufacturing company, he found that he enjoyed the process. Commerce included people working with other people to solve problems and create products that society values. He learned what it took to run a business, including leadership, managing people, working capital, and inventory control.

Ian also learned to trust his intuition about people. During his early time at Turner Uni-Drive, he worked and lived with Ernie Jones, whom he knew from the toy liquidation phase of his career. Ernie was an accountant of questionable character and received intel about a transaction going down in Rome with some defense contractors that he had worked with in the past. He convinced Ian to come with him as an ally, bodyguard, or both, and he asked Jay Nichols to accompany them so Turner Uni-drive would pay for the trip! The three of them jetted off to Rome and proceeded to the suite on the top floor of a swanky hotel where meetings were being conducted, room service was delivering piles of exotic food, and high-class Italian prostitutes were sashaying in and out of the bedrooms. These were unsavory people. The "business" men said they wanted to put together a company, and when Ian inquired about the name, they pointed to a bamboo cage near the mantle that held a stuffed Finch. "Finch & Co" they replied. It wasn't clear what they were trying to sell. There was talk of military equipment and working with Ferrari—they were all over the map. The "Finch & Co" comment placed Ian's instincts on high alert; he was convinced that they were con men and further suspected the men would not be able to pay for their hotel room and the Polizia would soon be involved. Ernie wanted to stay, but Dad didn't fancy a stint in an Italian jail, so he took a train to Paris and flew back to the United States. Ian could assess situations (and people) quickly and accurately and knew when to stay and when to get out. He would hone these instincts throughout his life, and they would serve him well throughout his career. He never told me what happened to Ernie. Ian was prepared for a real business opportunity, while Ernie saw the trip as a boondoggle. If you crossed Ian, that was the end. "Finch & Co" proved to be the end of his relationship with Ernie.

Bobbie

Around this time of his life, Jay Nichols was dating a tall, gorgeous woman named Patsy Darnaby. Her sister Barbara (equally as gorgeous as Patsy, and nicknamed Bobbie because her father thought she was going to be a boy) was at the Nichols' house one day and saw a photo of Ian with Jay's little sister, Del, which stopped her in her tracks.

"Who is *that*?" she asked.

"That's Ian, the mad Canadian. He's a wild man, have you not met him?" Jay replied.

At that moment, she knew that Ian was going to be an important part of her life. When they finally met in person, Bobbie described him as "the most electric, intelligent, interesting individual I had ever met in my life." By her account, he was equal measures brilliant, charming, funny, graceful (a great dancer because of the dancing lessons he had been forced to take as a child), and somewhat bizarre. He still had a Canadian accent and looked disheveled but was also uncommonly charismatic. She referred to him as a "wood nymph" with long hair and dandruff. Ian was an attractive combination of a transaction-oriented mind, a vibrant sense of playfulness, and childlike qualities. It was a whirlwind affair (including some romantic time spent in the *Pawhuska*), and the two eloped to Oklahoma in 1966 because Bobbie was just shy of being of legal age to marry (twenty-one) in the state of Kansas.

I was born shortly thereafter in April of 1967 while Ian was working his tail off at Turner Uni-Drive. The work at Turner Uni-Drive played to Ian's strengths. He was adept at identifying and stopping wasteful and inefficient practices, which resulted in major profitability gains that he later implemented at his company, Leucadia. Dad took walking the shop floor to heart, and he would often come home with metal shavings on his shoes, which would get embedded in the carpeting. Bobbie would get angry and say, "John's going to eat that stuff and we are going to have a real problem." One day she finally looked at him and said, "Ian why don't you get into something really dirty, like money." Jay had recently graduated from Harvard Business School (HBS), Clyde had told Ian that he wouldn't go anywhere in life unless he furthered his education, and with Bobbie's encouragement, Ian saw this as the next step for himself.

Harvard Business School (HBS)

As it turned out, all the things that made his disposition incongruent with the academic world and medical school were perfect for entrepreneurship. Once he determined that he was wired for business, his sense of self-worth escalated. He recognized his passion and drive for success but knew that he needed more formal instruction to further his career. At the time, HBS was the gold standard for business education, and his parents had done some graduate work at Harvard University, so he arranged for an interview. The interviewer said something along the lines of, *based on your transcript, Mr. Cumming, we are surprised you could even find your way to the admissions office.* The dean of admissions actually told him he wasn't "worthy to enter the admissions hall." Ian laughed and replied, "I will return every year and reapply until you let me in." He did apply despite the Dean's comments and was promptly denied and then rejected two more times. His will to beat the world into what he wanted it to be, however delusional and preposterous, eventually triumphed.

The dean of admissions at the time, along with the business school, was exploring a correlation between IQ, academic abilities, and future success in life. They concluded that persistence, more than other attributes, correlated highly with "success." After his third application, the admissions department finally said, "We think you will flunk but you are clearly persistent so we will give you a shot." Dad's audacious determination allowed him to set his sights on a goal and make it a reality. He moved with me and my mother to Cambridge when I was a toddler to attend HBS full-time, and my mom worked as a secretary at the university to pay our expenses. Ian's firsthand knowledge of working the factory floor and running the Turner Uni-Drive business allowed him to excel in the case method at HBS, and he blossomed in the competitive environment. A regular lecture experience where a professor droned on was not Ian's thing, but the case method was like nothing he had ever experienced. A hearty debate amongst his peers fascinated and inspired him.

One day during Ian's first year of business school, Edwin Marks, son of the early venture capitalist Carl Marks, made a presentation to the business students. Ian was intoxicated by what Ed said and by his demeanor—he was innovative and bold, but he also appeared kind of slovenly, like Ian. In him, Ian saw a parallel to his situation. Dad couldn't resist—the morning after the presentation, he showed up unannounced at Ed's hotel room. Marks came to the door in his towel. Ian said, "I want to work for you, *I want to be you*," and that is how he got his first job on Wall Street. His professors also gave him recommendations that resulted in the internship with Carl Marks. This situation required him to travel from Cambridge to New York while raising a kid and trying to get through HBS. Dad never balked at hard work, and he had finally found the thing that brought him joy and satisfaction. Consequently, he had tremendous energy and enthusiasm that fueled his ability to maintain a punishing schedule.

What Ian didn't know during this transitional time from reluctant medical student to business manager (because he had no relationship with his birth father) was that Fred McNeil was a successful businessman in his own right, who eventually led the Bank of Montreal. Ian had clearly inherited Fred's instincts for business, management, and leadership. Ian's history of feeling misunderstood and discarded by his family allowed him to love imperfect people and at the same time empower them. Dad had a gift for evaluating a person with about 95% accuracy within five minutes of meeting them, but he was also accepting, open-minded, and disarmingly playful, which made him a better human being and ultimately a better leader. The Mad Canadian had graduated to a serious American businessman.

Salt Lake City Pioneers

After graduating from HBS, Ian's internship at Carl Marks quickly turned into a full-time supervisory job. After Ian pleaded and cajoled with him, Joe Steinberg, a friend and fellow HBS graduate, agreed to join Ian at the firm. For several years, the two of them traveled the world seeking out undervalued investments. One of the companies Ian discovered during their travels was Terracor, a large land development company in SLC. Edwin Marks knew that if anyone could fix the faltering company, it was Ian. Dad was never a huge fan of Manhattan, and in Utah, he found an amazing outdoor lifestyle that appealed to him and represented what he wanted for his family. He also was attracted to the temperance that was a strong part of the Mormon community and culture. The sense of community, hard work, focus on family, and core values all felt grounding to Ian. At some point during these years, Ian recognized that SLC was where he wanted to raise his family, so he asked Ed Marks if he could buy Terracor. Marks agreed and helped arrange financing.

Dad moved Bobbie and me out to Utah in 1971 when I was about 4 years old, and we lived in one of the real estate developments that Terracor owned, called Stansbury Park near Tooele, Utah. A year later, my brother was born. Two important things in our lives came from Terracor; one was the family office on South Temple, and the other was the condo at the Turramurra Lodge at Snowbird. During our early years in SLC, we spent many a Monday evening having dinner with our Mormon neighbors, who were always kind and generous. The culture in Utah, largely dominated by Mormons, especially at that time, felt quite different to us after having lived in Kansas City and New York, and I supposed it's surprising in some ways that we were accepted so readily. Maybe we weren't and just didn't notice! Our mother must have noticed though, as it seemed to be the beginning of the end of that marriage.

Sometime in the mid-1970s, when I was around nine years old and my brother was only four, I remember hearing my dad loudly sobbing in the shower. It was heartbreaking to realize my dad, whom I revered and knew to be strong and unwavering, had totally broken down. I went to my parents' bedroom, my shoulders drooped, and I felt a heaviness in my body as I asked him what was wrong. He told me that our mother had left, and she was not coming back. He scooped me up in his arms and gave me the biggest, saddest hug. On that night, and many nights after that, my brother and I crawled into bed and simply held each other as we cried. This event solidified our partnership and support for each other at an early age; we are always there for each other and root for one another in everything we do. Apparently, Bobbie had gone back to Kansas for a high school reunion and rekindled a romance with her high school boyfriend. (This was the second time it had happened—we didn't know about the first) When she finally did return to Utah, she picked me up from Rowland Hall (the private school we attended in SLC) and told me that she and my dad had fallen out of love, and they were getting a divorce. It was the lowest I had ever seen my father. He was devasted because Bobbie had "stepped out on him" but also because it represented the end of our family as we knew it. Bobbie was a beautiful young beauty queen from Kansas, trying to be a mother in the middle of nowhere Utah. Dad was obsessed with his career and probably not spending enough time at home as a father and husband. The implications of his job on their relationship and our family are clearer in hindsight, but I was still resentful of my mother because she left our family.

That is when the gamesmanship began, and a drawn-out custody battle ensued. Dad hired the best divorce lawyer in the state of Utah; he wanted his boys. He wanted to keep the "three bears," as he called us, intact. And he believed Bobbie wasn't equipped to be a full-time mother of two rambunctious boys and he wasn't going to subject us to what he anticipated would be an unstable lifestyle with her and her boyfriend. Ultimately, I ended up meeting with the judge as a representative of "the boys."

"John, your mother and father have agreed to let you decide whom you want to live with, and you will also speak on behalf of your brother."

It seemed then and feels today like that was a lot to ask of a nine-year-old boy. Regardless, we just wanted Mom and Dad to stay together, but for reasons that I didn't fully understand at the time, we had to choose. I would pick my father. I took several deep breaths and tried to stand a bit taller as I spoke to the judge, "Mom doesn't enjoy being a mom as much as Dad enjoys being a Dad." Even as a child, I had understood this, and her leaving for Kansas for extended periods cemented the notion in my head. Mom erupted into tears saying that we had been brainwashed and that Dad told me what to say. It is probably true that I was somewhat programmed by my father to come to those conclusions, but I also felt like she was putting on a bit of a show. To this day, she complains that I am a robot programmed by my father.

My mother was and is a very charming, beautiful woman, but she was overwhelmed, as I'm sure many women of that generation were, with the responsibility of motherhood in her early 20's. I believe that my father seeking custody was certainly self-centered—he wanted the three bears to be together and support each other, something he felt he never had during his upbringing. But it was not an act of vengeance. He truly believed that we would be better cared for by him (when he was around) and nannies than by a mother who was obsessed with reliving her youth. She would probably not agree with this perspective and would feel unfairly criticized and judged. She had many wonderful attributes, but raising two high-energy boys did not match her strengths. Her family resembled something out of the book *Hillbilly Elegy*, so she didn't have a great role model for parenting, and she had no basis for understanding Dad's ambition and focus on wealth and power. Bobbie filed for divorce, and Dad fought for custody, but he was not a hostile co-parent. After the divorce, we spent time with our mother on the weekends, and I remember some loving moments with her, but Dad was our rock. Bobbie is very funny and fun to be around, but when she senses conflict, she reverts to emotional manipulation and blame. I remember some giggles and dancing to the Doobie Brothers at her house, but at nine years old, we had no conversations about her feelings after the divorce, so I can't speak to her version of events. Our relationship has remained at arm's length, and she does not have a relationship with my children, although she was invited to be in their lives. David and I have occasionally helped her financially when needed but our interactions over the years have been infrequent at best.

While Dad was, of course, jubilant that he had custody of his two boys, he was also in the sweet spot of his career and extremely busy building his company. Ian had befriended several people in the Mormon community, and when his marriage failed and he became a single father, he reached out to his friends at the Mormon Church looking for a nanny. Out of that process came Pierra Bellaviti, a nun from Vatican City who had converted to Mormonism. She was probably in her mid-fifties when she arrived at our home—practical, no-nonsense, exactly what you would picture an Italian nun to look like, minus the habit—and she essentially raised us for the next five years. She was a loving, nurturing, soul (the opposite of what we had experienced so far between my hard-nosed grandmother and my challenged mother), especially for my brother David who was so young. He describes her as his "four-foot-five-inch angel." She loved David and he loved her. She didn't love me quite as much because I was an unsettled "tween". She was so loved by our family that Ian gave her away at her wedding.

As two somewhat unruly boys who felt abandoned by their mother, we kept her working and posed daily challenges to her religiously calm demeanor. While Pierra was wonderful for us from a care and support perspective, her efforts as a cook and cleaner paled in comparison, and she was not much of a disciplinarian. She made some truly memorable meals such as hockey puck pork chops, meteor meatloaf, razor blade lasagna, and one of our favorites—mac and cheese with hot dogs. David and I also ate our weight in Eggo waffles during this time.

Over the next few years, Dad began dating and eventually married Annette Poulson, who became our stepmother. Annette (who was raised Mormon) had strong opinions about parenting. She believed in the pioneer way of things and that boys shouldn't require so much care. She was more concerned with hiring someone who could cook and clean, so Pierra was replaced by a lively, spirited young man named Antonio Benitas Reyes. Tony, as we called him, was from Spain. He was about five-foot-five-inches tall, had a thick mustache, longish black hair, permanent five o'clock shadow, and what would be referred to today as a unibrow. He wore caftans with sandals and was frequently visited by his gay friends. In our early teens, Tony would sneak us cigarettes and beer, later he taught me how to drive. I considered him more of a friend than a nanny. Nannies, for better or worse, were to become fixtures in our lives until we went away to boarding school. Annette and Ian had many disagreements about how we should be raised. She felt that we were indulged boys, and Ian didn't share her observations. Ian had found Susan the Shrink (as we jokingly called her) when he was trying to figure out the issues he had with his mother. Susan introduced us to a German therapist that we referred to as "The Goat." We had family therapy with The Goat and whenever he asked Dad how he thought we were doing, Ian would make a big SNAP motion with his fingers and say, "They are doing just GREAT!" I'm not sure therapy changed anything for me and David, but it gave Annette and Ian a neutral venue to air their grievances about us, so it seemed to help them.

Leucadia Is Born

Ian's training at Carl Marks and his insatiable hyperactivity led him to get involved with a public factoring[2] company based out of SLC called Talcott National Corporation. A Utah businessman named Brooke Grant had taken control of the failing company. He met Ian somehow through Terracor and asked Ian to see whether he could help Talcott through its troubles. No one could find their way around a balance sheet like Ian. He was the master, and the Talcott balance sheet and debt

---

[2] Factoring is a financial arrangement where a business sells its accounts receivable (invoices) to a third party, known as the factor, at a discount. This allows the business to access immediate cash flow rather than waiting for customers to pay their invoices.

structure were extremely complicated. Ian persuaded Joe Steinberg to fly out to Utah to help with Talcott as there were huge amounts of debt from more than fifty-six lenders. (Ian always liked to point out that Joe only had two jobs, and Ian recruited him for both of them!) Ian and Joe recognized that some aspects of the company were salvageable and could make money, but they would need some debt relief to move forward. Ian and Joe met with Dave McKown at Bank of Boston, one of the creditor banks. In layman's terms, the negotiation went something like this…

"If at the end of the day, the company goes into bankruptcy, the banks will be left holding the keys to a bunch of businesses that they don't understand. They'll never get their money back."

Ian and Joe mortgaged everything they owned, maxed out their credit cards, and signed their lives away to gather $3M. They had a plan that would bring the businesses back to life, but they needed time and forgiveness on the interest rates and terms, which would ultimately be more profitable for the banks in the long run. Dave McKown was impressed with the restructuring plan proposed by the two HBS MBAs and agreed to renegotiate the terms. Once the Bank of Boston agreed, the other banks fell in line. This interaction also resulted in Dave becoming a key advisor and friend to Ian and our family—a relationship that continued for decades until Dave's passing in 2021.

After Ian and Joe had begun to turn the business around, the Talcott owners returned to acquire the company name. Ian and Joe successfully sold the name to the Talcotts for more than the cost of the entire company, but it also put Ian and Joe on the spot to come up with a new name. Ian and Joe had been visiting Joe's house in Solana Beach, California, and they were driving north on the 101, on the phone with Steve Jacobs. He was their legal counsel from Weil, Gotshal, & Manges, a fancy law firm out of NYC that Ian referred to as wild gotcha millionaire because their billings were so high. They would bark out a name and Steve confirmed or denied availability. They tried multiple commonplace names like National Investment Company, but none were viable. Joe looked out the window and noticed they were driving through the small beach community near Encinitas called Leucadia.

He said to Ian, "How about Leucadia?"

Ian replied, "That's a great idea!"

Steve said, "What is a Leucadia?"

Regardless of its meaning, the name was available, and Leucadia was born in 1980. Over the next few years, Leucadia experienced rapid success. Unfortunately, Brooke Grant somehow felt like he got the short end of the stick during the Talcott negotiations, and he sued my dad personally for $5M. Ian was fighting to keep Terracor out of bankruptcy (which ultimately failed) and working long hours to grow Leucadia. I could see the stress on his face as he sat in his office, looking off into the distance, pinching his upper lip and his nose with one hand as his mind was engaged elsewhere. During the lawsuit, which went on for years, Ian wanted to impress upon the judge that he was not just another Wall Street flipper, he was also a father and upstanding member of the community. My brother and I would be "required" to appear at the hearings in our best dress clothes, sitting next to our stepmother, Annette, also in her conservative dress and serious red lipstick. I remember smelling Dad's sweat through his bespoke wool suit in the courtroom as the impending judgment bore down on him. In Ian's mind, he felt like he had simply played the capitalism game better than Brooke Grant did. In hindsight, he probably also might have felt a bit railroaded by the legal system being an outsider from Wall Street, facing off against a long-standing member of the Mormon community in SLC. Next to my mother leaving him, this was one of the hardest times in Ian's life. Eventually, they settled, costing Ian close to $4.5M. Obviously, this was not much of a win, but Leucadia would at last be free from legal disputes. This time, the Raven did not come away unscathed, his feathers were blackened a bit. To "celebrate" the settlement, Ian's good friend Dave Bragg, who at the time was Chairman of Oncology at the University of Utah and whose family had become ski buddies with ours over the years, appeared with baby bottles filled with martinis to begin Ian's healing process. Ian sat on the floor clutching his bottle with both hands and proceeded to giggle and tell stories with his dear friend. Even as a teenager, I appreciated the scene. Finally, free of lawsuits and bankruptcy proceedings, in 1984, Leucadia was able to continue its exponential growth with Ian and Joe at the helm.[3]

---

[3] "Leucadia National Corporation History," Funding Universe, accessed June 18, 2023, http://www.fundinguniverse.com/company-histories/leucadia-national-corporation-history.

To Create and Preserve Capital

Capital is King!

The more Ian learned, the more he realized that capitalism was the best system in the world because it afforded the most opportunity to people who took initiative; he always marveled at the resilience of Americans to get up, go to work, and fix any problem. I often heard him talk about being "Bigger, better, faster, stronger—carefully." For Ian, this illustrated the notion that the biggest and strongest would survive, and it was imperative to move quickly to act on opportunities, but not so quickly that he and Joe would have to depart from the values and mission set forth by their company. In other words, take a few deep breaths before giving the green light, and occasionally have the courage to do nothing. The worst possible outcome for any self-proclaimed capitalist is to lose money. At times, Ian suffered defeats while preserving his capital. After one failed deal, Barron's wrote, "It is obvious that Leucadia would rather be embarrassed than lose money." This was actually a compliment. Joe and Ian were smart, disciplined, and focused on objective success. Occasionally they would get involved in chasing a company that was trading at a range that made it an attractive acquisition target. After concentrated due diligence, they would often realize the value was not what they thought it was. Some companies would "close over" problems and move on with the deal, but Ian and Joe would not. They would either re-trade (try to renegotiate the offer) or leave the deal altogether, which could be somewhat embarrassing in the financial community. Dad was never hesitant to utilize new information to change the result of a negotiation. He often told me that all deals are controlled retreats. Everyone says yes in the beginning, but they eventually retreat backward as reality leaks into the equation.

Dad played hockey growing up in Canada, and he thought of capitalism like a hockey game: the boards had to be sturdy, and the rules needed to be clear so that there was no anarchy. Once those guidelines were established and the referees were on the ice, he played full contact. The ethics and the rules were necessary to protect the common good, so people didn't needlessly inflict harm on others. However, he played as hard and fast as he could within those boundaries, and his triumphs afforded him the ability to provide opportunities for others. Ian's primary objective was to create and preserve capital, and he had some strategic rules for investing that were evergreen.

- Rules for Investing
  1. Never pay too much
  2. Never invest in a business that you don't fully understand
  3. Never violate rule number 1
- Do business with people, not companies
- Banks are not reliable and are unpredictable partners
- Equity is gold, other things can be fixed
- Executives often don't know what is in the best interest of the company
- Conceal your capabilities, keep an air of mystery, and then jump quickly to act on an opportunity

Truffle Pig and Junkyard Dog

Professor Howard Stevenson, Sarofim-Rock Baker Foundation Professor Emeritus at Harvard Business School, famously defined entrepreneurship as "the pursuit of opportunity beyond resources controlled."[4] *Forbes* magazine once described Professor Stevenson as HBS's "lion of entrepreneurship" in a 2011 article, and Ian learned a great deal from him, and he ended up being a great friend in addition to an influential professor. When Ian and Joe started, they had very few resources, so they had to rely on other capabilities to achieve success. They were creative and discerning in how they sought out opportunity. Often, they were looking through other people's corporate rubbish to discover and cultivate a hidden gem. Ian used to call himself a "truffle pig" because of his endless curiosity to search out possibilities that others couldn't see and turn them into something valuable. With a playful grin, he would tap his nose and snort, "I could smell it; I'm a truffle pig."

Much like the shapeshifting Raven, Dad maintained a low profile in public, which allowed him to identify and vet undervalued companies or ideas that he could then turn around with his team. Ian never allowed his photo in the annual company reports, nor did he allow the news media to take his photo. It was part of his schtick as the elusive "deals guy." His anonymity allowed Leucadia to be a preferred buyer for many deals, in part because owners were confident that they wouldn't be reading about the turnaround in the media. For many years, the public viewed him as a mysterious, hard-nosed businessman. Finally, a reporter got hold of a photo and described him as looking like Captain Kangaroo, the lead character in a children's show that aired on weekday

---

[4] *Entrepreneurship: A Working Definition* by Tom Eisenmann, January 10th, 2013.

mornings for more than thirty years. The playful and warm (yet somewhat paunchy) Captain, dressed in colorful clothes, would teach life lessons to kids through lighthearted interaction with puppets. This comparison always stood out in my mind as it captured the playful nature of my father, which was incongruent with the cut-throat corporate raider he sometimes played at work.

Many times, Dad would be looking out the window, lost in his world and it was hard to get his attention. His leg would be rapidly going up and down as my brother and I would jump in front of him flailing our arms and yelling, "Hello! Hello!" When I asked what he was thinking about, he would answer "I was leaping tall buildings." Translation: he was exploring the gestalt of opportunities that were on his radar on any given day. He was often ten steps ahead of everyone else (or at least me) in putting together the Rubik's cube of business strategy. If an organization seemed broken or undervalued, he would consider the circumstances in a greater context, "How did this happen? Can it be fixed? If so, can we take advantage of it? What does the team look like? What hole does this fill in the market?" He had a clever business mind and could unearth value where most could only skim the surface. His ability to ask the right questions and think on a multi-dimensional level was a marvel to behold.

Ian had an unmatched work ethic, which is critical if you go down the entrepreneurial path, and even more so if you aspire to build something enduring. He often referred to himself as a "junkyard dog;" he prided himself on being able to work harder and longer than anyone else, endure more pain, and if necessary, chew the leg off an unwanted transgressor. Dad worked impossibly long hours, maintained an exhausting travel schedule, consistently synthesized a vast amount of information, and always had multiple projects going at the same time. For most people, it would have been a debilitating and unthinkable schedule, but Ian thrived in this environment.

Where he also stood out was in his capacity to go through the process, take charge, and with only a reasonable guestimate of the situation, make a decision. Ian would often say, "I am often wrong, but never in doubt," which seems to be a defining characteristic of entrepreneurs. Ian might have been wrong, but someone had to decide, and if it happened to turn out badly, he would accept responsibility, let it roll off, and move on to the next thing. He had a tremendously high tolerance for pain and a short memory—something he would pass on to me and that would serve me well for most of my life.

Great Leaders

Dad's office, which he acquired during the Terracor days and became Leucadia HQ in SLC, is along the route my brother David and I would walk home from school. Since we weren't eager to go home and do homework supervised by our nanny, we would often stop by to visit Dad. The office is in the David Keith Mansion and Carriage House, which was designed by the SLC architect Frederick Albert Hale and built in the late 1800s; it is one of the few remaining mansions on South Temple. The first floor was awash in wall-to-wall green carpeting, and the walls were and still are covered in heavily lacquered dark wood paneling. The space was at once imposing and elegant. Curated art adorned the walls, and ornate mantels framed the fireplaces; it felt like you were walking into a museum. Ian loved the decorum of it, it reminded him of a time when business was more formal than it is today. For a guy who was often cheerful and playful, he had an incurable addiction to fancy suits and outdated office formality.

Ian traveled a great deal, but when he was home, we were grateful and wanted to be around him as much as possible. Dad was always happy to see us, but he would continue working, and as long as we were quiet, we could stay. Some of my earliest memories of Dad involved playing in his office while he was on the phone or in a meeting. I believe all those years of visits to the office as he was doing business taught me the characteristics of leadership: honesty, integrity, directness, sincerity, humility, and humor. I listened to his intonation and rhythm and noted the authenticity of his communications, I can only hope that I absorbed some of these traits. The openness and warmth that made him a great human being also made him a great leader.

Dad had a lot of innate leadership talent, but he also learned the language of management from his time at HBS. Many of the leadership principles he applied came from his favorite professor, Dr. Chris Christensen, one of the leading thinkers on business strategy and a creator of the business case teaching method. Ian treasured the education he received at HBS. He often shared the notes he had taken during his last class with Professor Christensen. They were so important to him that he had them laminated and carried them at all times.

Ian learned that one of the most important attributes for leaders to have is a sincere curiosity about the people with whom they work. He believed that you couldn't fully comprehend the numbers until you had a deep understanding of the people and places that produce those numbers. *("Do business with people, not companies.")* Human beings are the backbone of all companies and trusting one another is a prerequisite for good business. Dad maintained that personal concern was the greatest human motivator, and he would remind us that "WWI soldiers were willing to charge enemy lines if they had a sergeant who worried about them having dry socks."

Ian adhered to the maxim, "Lead, follow, or get out of the way." Everyone has their role, and if a leader is elected/established and is willing to take on that responsibility, then others should fall in line. Dad sought out employees who were "honest, hard-working, and smart, in that order." He valued intelligence, integrity, energy, and judgment far more than academic degrees or industry resumes, and above all, he learned to love and manage imperfect people. Ian had a way of helping

45

you see that you were capable of more than you thought. And because you didn't want to disappoint him, you would push yourself to accomplish more than you would have without his insistence.

According to Professor Christensen, "Great leaders can do extraordinary things with ordinary people." Leaders must have the ability to absorb enormous hurt and disappointment and be resilient enough to accept it and move on. A leader doesn't necessarily have to be the smartest person in the room, but they do have to be self-confident enough to own the failures, share the victories, and celebrate the success of others. Ian was brilliant, empathetic, curious, humorous, and warm on the individual level, but always with the macro context in mind. The emotional well-being of the team was paramount to the overall health of the company and the ultimate goal of growing and preserving capital. But if one of the team members didn't perform and their presence was damaging to the greater community, then the priority was clear—the leader had to step up and do what was needed. "Be charitable when people fail if they have done their best—but often with a good severance package."

Ian's respect and admiration for Professor Christensen and his perspectives about leadership are forever represented in the building he established that bears his name, The C. Roland Christensen Center. The center is designed to help facilitate hands-on, real-world learning for students at the University of Utah, David Eccles School of Business.

Don't Fall in Love with Refrigerators

Ian and Joe were early pioneers of the LBO (leveraged buyout) strategy, and they were often referred to as "Corporate Raiders." Inherent in this business model was the fact that they sometimes capitalized on other people's failures. They would buy stock or debt that they believed was misvalued and take over companies. They would then hold them, fix them up, or sell off the parts for a price greater than the whole. Usually, this involved languishing stock, bad management, deficient strategy, or some combination of the three. The interest rates of the 1980s also worked to their advantage. In 1980, the prime rate was 15.2%, and a lot of companies couldn't manage their debt load and were forced to sell or refinance. Ian and Joe earned a reputation on Wall Street as "savvy young investors." For someone like Ian who had considerable instincts, and who was resourceful and determined, the timing couldn't have been more perfect. Ian and Joe were able to ride those interest rates down to zero over the next thirty-five years, which provided significant advantages. Ian and Joe would often speculate about "Ten Bangers"— this was an investment that was so cheap, that they would make ten times their money. This was the ultimate truffle pig prize, and they had a few of them. When it happened, Ian would get very excited and do one of his little jigs.

Another tactic the two men used was something called greenmailing. If they couldn't get control by buying the stock, they would threaten a hostile takeover. The targeted company agrees to a "greenmail" whereby they pay a premium on the stock so the takeover company will leave them alone. On the back staircase of his office in Salt Lake, Dad had a wall full of checks he received from this effort. Again, in Dad's world, this was just business. Ian was quite ebullient and optimistic, but also realistic—he was playing by the rules, but he was playing full contact to win. Ian and Joe saw an opportunity to create value and they took it; those companies had done something to get in an unfavorable position, and Leucadia was happy to profit from it. The shrewd Raven is not afraid to do what needs to be done. People openly criticized them for being "bottom feeders," or for profiting from others' misfortune, but they didn't care. Ian was always comfortable in his skin, unapologetic, and as long as he didn't lie, cheat, or steal, his conscience was clear. The objective goal of creating capital brought him joy and far outweighed the subjective or emotional aspect of a business. Leucadia's philosophy was straightforward: they were shrewd, savvy capitalists who specialized in distressed situations. They were focused on building shareholder value and minimizing taxes. Profits would come.

Dad and Joe were always on the road searching for "undervalued assets" that they could add to Leucadia's holdings. During one of their excursions, they came across a struggling company that manufactured refrigerators. The two partners were objective-minded, HBS-educated, discerning businessmen, but they also had a little act they did during these negotiations. They would bicker with each other and disagree in front of the management team or seller's representative; it was a disarming tactic that led to openness and trust throughout the negotiation. The conversation would usually proceed to impartial measures of shareholder equity, working capital, replacement value, operating margins, performance trends, etc. Ian and Joe used their business school training to quantify the opportunity in the context of their investment strategy, which was hunting for truffles to grow their equity.

During the discussion, one of the target company's managers got frustrated and said, "It is obvious that the two of you don't understand the product."

Dad rolled his eyes and replied, "They are fucking refrigerators."

Translation: don't get carried away with the subjective, always maintain a focus on objective goals and measures. Discipline in this area dramatically improves the probability of success. Ian's unshakable objectivity led him on an amazing journey, and his success gave him objective and subjective value. Interestingly, even though he taught me not to fall in love with a product, my career has largely been driven by the subjective. In the outdoor industry, there are times when you need to do both. Knowing the difference, and when to focus on which, has been imperative for me, and Ian taught me the difference between the two.

Passion and Patience

Two distinguishing characteristics of Dad's identity were his impulsive curiosity and almost childlike enthusiasm for life. He always had a twinkle in his eye, reflecting the passion that blazed inside him. Ian had an insatiable appetite for "new information," that verged on the neurotic. At all times, he had five or six giant satchels overflowing with reports, data, magazines, articles, newspapers, etc. It was through learning and synthesizing information that he was able to become successful almost beyond what he had imagined for himself.

One of the photographs of Ian that I find descriptive of his personality, is of him standing in the middle of a street in his favorite city, London, near a manhole with a cone next to it. A worker has climbed about halfway out of the access shaft. Dad is next to the cone, clearly where he is not supposed to be, overcome by curiosity, bending down to peer into the hole, trying to figure out what is going on beneath the surface. It looks like he is about to question the man ascending from below about what he is doing. Ian's humility and respect for people from all walks of life caused him to treat a laborer the same way he would treat a CEO. There was always something fresh to learn, whether it came from an HBS professor or a man working under the street. Every experience changes the last one; the world is constantly transforming. Nobody knows everything, and we should continually be open to new information. As such, Ian had astounding intellectual plasticity. He could almost effortlessly take in new information and incorporate it into his thinking and decision-making. New information never undermined his core values, but it might quickly shift his perspective on new opportunities.

In the enigma that is Ian, at the same time that he could be flexible with absorbing information and acting on it, he could also have incredible patience not to act.

Ian had many traits that distinguished him from other businessmen, but none was more important than his ability to exercise patience. As discussed, the premise of Ian and Joe's company, Leucadia, was to uncover and buy undervalued assets, fix them, and sell them for a profit. This was their mission, and they stuck to it monastically; buying the trends was not part of their approach.

Truffle pigs can sometimes go a long time before finding the next perfect, fragrant mushroom. And Ian and Joe would go for extended periods without doing any investing. They did miss some of the general market upturns during their careers, but they remained emphatically loyal to their core expertise. It was frustrating, but they knew if they forced something or overpaid for an asset, the odds of them succeeding would decrease. Their ambition to NOT lose money outweighed any inclination to follow the investment fads swirling around them. At times, the symphony was blaring, everyone was dancing, and Joe and Ian sat on the sidelines thinking "Well that looks fun, but it is not what we do." They demonstrated resolve and clarity about their principles and were dedicated to avoiding what we now call "mission creep." As much value is created by *not doing* as doing; the advantage of this type of discipline cannot be overemphasized. The "strength to do nothing" is one of the main things that helped them to stand out from other business leaders and allowed them to build a profitable, enduring conglomerate over thirty-five years even during the most notable recession in recent history.

Unapologetic

My father frequently told me, "The truth is the most powerful weapon in the world." Most people can't handle the truth, but Ian and his partner Joe used it as a competitive edge in their business dealings. Their ability to be authentic created a sense of trust among their partners and executives. In the letters that Dad wrote to his shareholders over the years, he didn't sugarcoat returns or results; he was honest about the investments that didn't work out, excited about the profitable ones, and he was humorous and thoughtful throughout his communication. While the bulk of the document was financial, in each paragraph and for every company he spoke highly of the company executives as well as the skilled workers. He outlined the issues going on in the larger geopolitical climate, but always within the context of how human beings would interact with each other and the world.

When Ian met with people, he was inclusive, genuine, and unapologetic for who he was, and therefore accepting of who they were. His natural curiosity allowed him to easily find mutual discoveries and common ground. His demeanor was intoxicating to people. He was childlike in many of his mannerisms and interactions—he just loved business, and his enthusiasm shined through. At the same time, if anyone lied to him, that was the end of it, as evidenced by his abrupt departure from Italy during the Ernie Jones debacle early in his career. He had no tolerance for anyone who lacked integrity. He did business with people, not companies, and he led with his heart and a powerful level of veracity and decency.

Ian said that companies are like big families and that there should not be secrets in an organization or a family. Just like children can sense things about their parents, employees know the intent of leadership. You can't try to hide from them. There can be confidential information, but any "secrets" are likely to get out; if you understand that, then you don't do anything that requires being secretive. Sometimes we aren't proud of our actions, but we are all flawed human beings, and we have to own our problems. Living in this way produces a certain amount of power and freedom.

Dad did not care much about what other people thought of him, and he did not put on airs. I remember sitting in a meeting with him when I was a young adult and watching him picking his nose. And I mean really digging up there, he wasn't trying to hide it. I shook my head in disbelief. After the meeting, I reprimanded him, "Dad you cannot pick your nose in the middle of a business meeting or in front of other people!"

He and his longtime friend, Bud Scruggs, would get great joy out of heading into a McDonald's in their bespoke London-made suits and wolfing down a couple of Big Macs and fries. One time he stage-whispered to Bud, "THIS is why I never allow my photo to be published. No one here knows who we are, and no one cares!"

Bud would sometimes try to curb Ian's boorish side, "A man of your stature and place in the world should not swear so much!"

Ian would respond, "Fuck You Scruggs."

As long as people knew he was an upstanding citizen and ethical businessman, the rest didn't matter. He was completely true to the version of himself that he wanted to be.

A Sucker for Conviction

Dad was attuned to loyalty and conviction; he valued people who were all in. Ian met his partner, Joe Steinberg at HBS, and they went on to have a thirty-five-year partnership. Upon arrival at HBS, students are assigned to a specific "section"—a group of students with whom they will complete the required curriculum. Ian was reading the HBS student newspaper (*The Harbus*) and there was an article about a student in the other section (Joe), who was trying to put a group together to buy Boston City Hall, which was in bankruptcy at the time. Dad's first thought was, I need to meet this guy—he is obviously really smart, ambitious, and audacious! Ian was aware of his strengths but also knew that we all needed help. Given the elegance of Joe's restructuring plan for City Hall, Ian thought that Joe's skill set could be a perfect complement to his own. Together, they had the potential to create a powerful entity in the world of finance. It took a few years, but they formed a partnership that was characterized by mutual respect and expertise. In Ian's conceptualization of capitalism as a hockey game, Ian was the flashy winger and Joe was the obsessive goaltender. They were yin and yang, but both were brilliant negotiators, and they never did a deal unless both of them were enthusiastic about it.

In Dad's last letter to his shareholders, Joe and Ian described their lifelong loyal partnership as one in which they had "unfailingly stood by one another in times of heartache, health, and personal challenges." They wrote, "We trust one another and respect the value of our differing skills, interests, and intuition."

When Dad and I eventually started working together, he was skeptical about the outdoor apparel industry—this was not his wheelhouse, after all. As he watched me stay focused on it, and we learned more, I could see him reevaluating his position. He could make decisions based on his gut, but I had to justify everything. He would do things instinctually, yet he would battle with me over decisions until he saw the fire in my eyes, and then he would let me go ahead with my vision. He used to call me a tough old boot because I wouldn't back down. This inevitable butting of heads created an energy and angst inside of me that made me determined to succeed. I had to fight for what I wanted, but it was hard to fight with my father. He was a smart, stalwart opponent and we would often go on until I banged on the table or found the guts to put my foot down. Finding an agreement with someone who was so objectively driven and intelligent and who was also your Dad was hard; if you weren't willing to battle with him and demonstrate your conviction, he didn't see you as a worthwhile business interest. He pushed me to my limit more times than I care to count, but I understand now why he did it. If you are going to bet on a horse, you want to bet on the one who is snorting and pushing the gate and looks the most formidable, because he is the one who is going to give it all to win the race. Bud Scruggs summarized Ian's theories about conviction as follows:

- If it was your hunch vs. Ian's hunch, he won.
- If it was your facts vs. Ian's hunch, you argued.
- If it was your conviction . . . he admitted that he was a "sucker for conviction."

Kermit the Gulfstream

As Dad's company experienced exponential growth, his travel schedule became increasingly hectic. Commercial flying took a lot of time, and time was money. He subscribed to the joking adage that if it floats, flies, or fl@#s, rent it—but "if you can't, buy it used!" (as a disclaimer, Ian never paid for sex). He dabbled with several smaller planes that could only fly for a couple of hours at a time. Flying back and forth from NYC with a headwind could take upwards of eight hours sometimes. Because he traveled so much, he referred to himself as a *Homo sapiens* tube dweller. Dad saw other businessmen fly private and became obsessed with the idea of owning a private jet. Like everything else in his life, he compulsively studied them and learned everything he could about the various specs and functions of airplanes, the payloads, block times, speed range, dispatch reliability, parts availability, maintenance, etc. First, he bought a small used Cheyenne; second, a slightly smaller but faster Falcon 10; third, a Citation Three; and finally, a used Gulfstream 2 that he bought from a Sheik. He was bemused by the interior décor and the smell. Apparently, the Sheik was into falcons and had transported his birds using the plane. Ian finally bit the bullet and purchased a Gulfstream 550, fresh from the manufacturer; he was so proud of this achievement and milestone in his career, though he never spoke of it publicly. In your mind, you are probably picturing an elegantly appointed private jet as you see in the movies, with a quiet cabin and freshly prepared meals served by a flight attendant at your beck and call.

Kermit the Gulfstream was a different animal. In typical Ian fashion, he found a tax loophole that allowed for 100% depreciation if the plane was flown for fifty hours before the end of the calendar year. The government, especially in the state of New York, was always trying to extract more tax from him, so whenever he could legally reduce his tax bill, he took advantage. The problem was that there was no way to have the plane completed in time to get the tax benefit, so he took delivery of it unfinished. Ian figured this wasn't much of a sacrifice in exchange for multiple millions in tax savings. The plane arrived with only the primer paint it came with, which was a dull chartreuse green, correlating quite closely to the beloved puppet, Kermit the frog. Hence, the nickname. He had two chairs bolted into it and added some lead weights to the floor for ballast. There was no soundproofing, so passengers had to wear noise-canceling headphones just to hear their thoughts. Conversation was not an option. The only bathroom was a camping toilet that someone picked up at REI, and nary a flight attendant was lurking in the hollow vessel. Ian planted himself in there like a stoic soldier heading off for deployment. He would recruit people to come with him; he flew anyone who needed to get somewhere quickly, and by the time Kermit's fifty hours were up, the primer was worn off and the aircraft looked like it had been through a war.

Ian would pull into the FBO (flight-based operations) of an airport where all of the other private flyers were, exit the glaringly green Kermit with his head held high, a satisfied smile on his face, in his custom-made Saville Row threads and shiny wingtip shoes. I can only imagine what the other high-powered execs thought. Paying full retail was something that went against Dad's core beliefs. If he had to suffer a little bit to be able to say he got a great deal, so be it. He also saw the plane as something of a perk that made up for the less pleasant parts of being the boss. He shared the company's success with everyone, and he bravely absorbed the failures on his own, but "the plane belongs to the chairman." He wanted the power, convenience, and luxury that came with owning a jet, but he wanted it to be within his rules of capitalism. Never overpay! As for Ian's partner, Joe Steinberg? Joe was joyfully speeding through the sky in the jet you pictured earlier.

The Brass Ring

Dad often referred to the concept of the Brass Ring. You jump and leap and strive to get the ring and then when you get it, you throw it over your shoulder. All of that energy disappears as soon as it is in your grasp, and then you start hunting for the next ring. You do the same things over again, leaping, striving, reapplying the same level of commitment, and you don't care about the sacrifice. You fret and strain and bleed until you figure out how to reach it. This is the disease that entrepreneurs have, and I inherited it from my father. It is a wonderful, unique trait, but a preposterous insanity at the same time. I often think of it as the beautiful neurosis that makes the world go around.

In late 2007, Dad and I, along with some of the family, were gathered at our old condo at the Marriott at PCMR getting ready to go skiing. Ian's phone rang, and he of course compulsively answered it. I was close enough to hear the conversation,

"Hi Ian, it's Warren Buffet calling."

The corners of Ian's mouth turned up a bit in a faint smile as he responded, "Hello Warren, what can I do for you?" He played it totally cool, but I could see that he was flattered. Ian and Joe had been looking at buying a commercial mortgage company called Capmark, but the deal required more capital than they had on hand at the time.

Warren continued, "I've been a shareholder of Leucadia for a while, watching what you and Joe have been doing. Capmark is a good deal, but it seems like it might be kind of big for you. If we combine your brains and my capital, we could make something great." When he got off the phone, I parroted back something Dad often said to me, "Some things are worth more than money, huh?" Berkadia was formed in early 2009 with Warren, Joe, Ian, and Berkshire's CFO, Mark Hamburg, all sitting on the board of directors together. It's not every day that one of the world's richest men calls your cell phone and proposes doing a deal together. One would think this would have been the pinnacle of Ian's career, but he was out looking for deals the very next day—no such thing as the top.

The Enigma

During his incredibly successful career, Ian was a creature of diligence and planning. His personal attributes were often contrary to his business profile—offering yang to his yin, amusement to his seriousness, impulse to restraint, and adventure to balance the intellectual drive.

The Power of Family

Ian's stepfather, John, always said that neurosis was the mother of all success, and this was particularly true for Ian; his complicated relationship with his parents ultimately drove him to work harder. While his mother and adoptive father loved him, they were often condescending and critical, which led to a thorny relationship. At one point as an adult, Dad reached out to his biological father, Fred McNeil, and was discouraged to find that Fred had another family with three children and didn't want Ian to be part of his life. Dad was sad and hurt, but he let it roll off his back. He continued with a "What's Next?" attitude, but I often wondered if this hurt him more than he let on.

Fred passed away when Ian was in his late fifties and until that time, Ian had had no contact with Fred or his family, per Fred's instructions.

However, upon Fred's passing, Ian read in his obituary that donations could be made to the MS foundation to benefit his daughter, Marie, who had the autoimmune disease. Ian made a sizable donation, and as Marie was sifting through the donations and writing thank you notes, she saw one from the Cumming Foundation and asked her mother about it. Her mother told her the truth but made her swear not to tell her brothers. Marie felt like an injustice had been done, so she reached out to Ian to see if he wanted to meet her. She left a message with his assistant, and after he read the message, his mouth fell open and he started shaking as he brought the note to Annette. He called Marie that night and they talked for an hour and a half; a wide smile spread across his face as they learned about each other after almost a lifetime of being apart. Marie recollects, "We both felt the connection immediately. I just knew this person right away." They experienced an immediate bond, one that Ian never felt with his other family members, and Marie was able to provide some of the unconditional love that Ian had craved throughout his life. They were similar—both smart, charismatic, entrepreneurial business leaders with great people and communication skills. They were so similar in fact, that they often fought as siblings do. Their relationship remained strong until his death, and Ian's last trip before he died was to visit Marie. We didn't think it was in his best interest to travel then, but he was emphatic that he needed to say goodbye to his half-sister. Even though they only knew each other for twenty-five years or so, she was a special soul in his life. On a similar note, although Ian and his mother had their differences, during her last month of life, Ian did his duty and was there with her almost every day. They reconciled and were on good terms before she passed away. Ian and his half-brother David, who we affectionately refer to as "Gruncle," bought Granny a nice apartment in Vancouver toward the end of her life, and Ian would send the private jet to get her every once in a while. Ironically, she seemed less judgmental about Ian being in "commerce" after she was able to enjoy the perks of wealth. Gruncle once commented, "If only we had known that all it took was $1M to buy her an apartment to be nice to us, we would have done it long ago."

Papa Bear

The judgment and lack of nurturing Dad experienced during his formative years fueled his obsession with hard work, but it also made him cognizant of the need to provide a loving environment for David and me.

He used to say that he was born with a great feminine energy, or "anima" that overflowed for us and our families. He never came into the room without extending his arms, saying, "Come here!" and giving us a big, sincere hug. He was always happy to be with us, and we had many adventures together skiing, climbing, and traveling the world. Moreover, the Dad we knew at home would occasionally break into song and dance (although he had a terrible voice). He would jump up and point his toes like a ballerina and do a little twirl, which was preposterous, self-deprecating, and silly. *Look at me, I'm fat but I can still dance!* He could light up a room with his positive, playful energy and we were drawn to it like moths to a flame. Then, he would leave again, traveling for work, cooking up deals, and his absence created a glaring contrast that we felt acutely. Even though we had some great nannies, they were not our parents, and they could never come close to being as entertaining or as enthusiastic as our father. He was our everything.

That is not to say, that we did not have discipline. When we were little, Dad approached parenting a little like business; we were allowed to play hard and fast within the boundaries, but if we stepped over, there was hell to pay. I remember one particular incident after our mother left. I was an unsupervised, rascally, little boy. For some unknown reason, I decided to light the fence on fire in the backyard. Dad came home from work, lifted me by the arm, and practically threw me into my room. Then he came in and slowly unhooked his belt and unthreaded it from his pants. He doubled it up and pulled it taught in a dramatic show of authority that only heightened my crying in anticipation of the punishment. Dad had a fairly old-school upbringing from his adoptive father, John, and I'm sure he got the belt a few times. Dad spanked us when we were naughty but given the more serious nature of this crime on my part, he notched up the punishment. I fought like a cat in a trap and wailed throughout the event. My brother, on the other hand, only got the belt once or twice. Dad later told me that when he hit David with the belt, he didn't utter a peep, and the lack of reaction startled him, so he never did it again.

Dad's dedication to his business made his physical presence scarce, which negatively impacted us, but it also made us appreciate the times he was around even more. He would always take our phone calls—he would even interrupt a meeting to talk to us about anything we needed. There was never a doubt about how much he loved us. Following Dad's example, David and I have prioritized each other and our children throughout our own lives. We always answer the phone when our children call—it is the most critical thing. And we always answer the phone for each other. Family is our first consideration.

We spent some of our most treasured times together as a family at Snowbird. Dad loved to try new things and he gave his sons the opportunity and confidence to go with him. When we were quite young, Dad was still working in New York while we lived in Salt Lake City. He would fly in on Thursday night from New York, and we would be in bed, sometimes pretending to be asleep, when he arrived. He would scoop up my brother and me, carefully put us in the back of the car, and drive us up to Snowbird. He had a place in what is now called The Inn, but back then it was called the Turramurra Lodge. His smell was always immediately soothing to me. He smelled like he had completed a hard workout. It wasn't acrid or like BO; it was sweet and warm. For me, it symbolized safety and reassurance, like crawling into a familiar den.

When we woke up in the morning, inevitably he would be on the phone with Joe or somebody, working on a "deal." He made us breakfast while on the phone and David and I got into our long underwear—I put on my long Johns and David put on his long Davids. We often wore the same clothes—Dad never played favorites and went to great efforts to treat us equally (and it was probably easier to just buy two of everything). While still on the phone, Dad would point out the window and mouth to us, "Meet me at the plaza at noon." We would race to grab our stuff and ski our little brains out until we met Dad at the Forklift for lunch. Sometimes, if he had a conflict, there would be a note on the chalkboard at the bottom of the lift, "John and David— meet your Dad at 2 pm."

One of my most vivid memories is when Dad took David and me to explore Great Scott, an expert-level chute in the cirque. We were certainly not double black diamond skiers at that point, but that didn't stop us, as usual, Dad was curious and 100% committed. Dad was methodical when it came to business, but his outdoor adventures were a bit more haphazard and unplanned, like the frivolous Raven. Reflecting on the scene, it seems kind of humorous now, but it wasn't at the time. My brother and I were looking over the cornice of one of the most iconic runs at Snowbird, paralyzed with fear. David squeezed his eyes shut, and my mind was filled with apprehension. Dad was wearing his industrial yellow one-piece ski suit with a black and yellow striped vest over the top that made him look like a bumblebee. Dad (perhaps because of his Canadian roots) seemed impervious to the cold, and he never skied with a hat on. He looked around and said, "John, you go first, you can do it." I let go of the breath I had been holding and vaulted myself down the hill. I made several rough turns and looked back up toward my father. He was lying down on the cornice with my little brother dangling from his hand as he lowered him over the edge. We had our doubts (David for sure—he was only six years old at the time), but the fact that Dad knew we could do it gave us the courage (as children) to survive and eventually conquer an expert run at one of the most difficult mountains in the country. Just like Dad knew I would survive the Grand Teton and that I was strong enough to speak to the judge about custody, his will and confidence allowed us to get down that chute.

Ian was dedicated to making all of us master skiers, and this was part of the journey. He gave us the self-confidence we needed to leap into the unknown, and we all shared in the sense of invincibility one experiences after doing something challenging. Dad was right; we could do it. He pushed us out of our comfort zone, maybe a little too much at times, but he always had our backs, and David and I had each other's backs. These experiences produced a phenomenal family bond and indelible memories, which is ultimately what led me to pursue a career in the ski/outdoor industry later in life. I believe that my life was enormously enriched in the mountains. I learned independence, mastery of a sport, and gained a huge appreciation for the Snowbird community that helped raise us and the breathtaking nature that surrounded us. Although I absolutely loved the time with my father in the mountains, it seemed incompatible with his day job, which sparked and then fueled my animosity toward Wall Street. I knew at an early age that I did not want to do what he did.

Loyal to Friends and Family

In addition to being in a business partnership for many years with Joe, Ian was married to Annette Poulson (an ICU nurse) for more than forty years. He always said, "Hire engineers and marry nurses!" He believed that nurses were reliable, decisive, and highly competent individuals who could also be caring. Engineers were good at solving problems. As an outsider, we can only ever know a fraction of what goes on in a marriage, but Ian and Annie's bond was a strong one. After his first two marriages, he needed someone with confidence and with whom he shared mutual respect. He admired Annette's strength, resolve, work ethic, and commitment to women's issues. Her independence, resilience, sense of adventure, and intelligence made her a good life partner for Dad.

Ian also believed in keeping his contracts. Marriage is the ultimate commitment between two people, and any commitment implies a certain level of hard work will be required. Ian and Annette were both determined to stay together, through the good and the bad, in sickness and in health, and keep their vows to each other. While I did not view Dad as the best expert on marriage, he did teach David and me to choose wisely when it came to our life partner and to honor our contract.

Ian treasured his friendships outside of work as well. Steve Swindle was one of the friends he made in SLC that he was close with until his death. Dad needed a lawyer, and Steve worked for Van Cott, Bagley, a prestigious Utah firm. Over the years they became incredibly close friends, and our families often traveled and spent time together. Steve and Ian had similar interests and values and even looked like brothers. They wore the same glasses, combed their hair the same way, wore similar styles of suits, and they both had a twinkle in their eye. While Dad always had a bit of an edge, a sort of underlying competitiveness to him, Steve was loving, accepting, and nurturing. He has been and still is like an uncle to me, and we chat often. Steve was a loyal friend throughout Ian's life, particularly through his mild cognitive impairment (MCI) diagnosis and eventual decline.

Ian was loyal to his business, family, and friends, but he was also loyal to himself. High achievement and hard work are what made him happy, and without those things in his life, he would not have been the best version of himself when he was with his family. He traveled and worked a great deal, which took him away from his family and friends. But when he was with us, he demonstrated absolute love and dedication. He knew that he would not have been a good father or husband if he sacrificed the passion that drove him, the essence of who he was.

The Golden Rule

Even as he wholeheartedly embraced capitalism, Ian still had the value system that was ingrained in him from his early days in Canada with his socialist parents. That value system made him acutely aware that with capitalist opportunities came the responsibility to look after the common good.

Ian always had a strong moral compass and a solid sense of right and wrong. All of these things led to him being heavily involved in his community: he was campaign manager for several local politicians, he served on the Utah Athletic Commission, he was on the board of the University of Utah Hospital System, and eventually, he was on the State of Utah Board of Regents, to name a few. All of this made him a very well-connected figure in the state, and he was often in the Governor's office giving or receiving advice.

He was also widely respected and accepted in the Mormon community. Robert Hales, one of Dad's close friends and an Apostle in the Mormon Church, often met with Ian over lunch to philosophize and exchange ideas. Ian and Bob's relationship reached back to their days at Harvard. Ian joked with Bob that he would consider joining the Mormon church on two conditions: first he needed a tithing exemption, and second, he demanded to be in charge of the Church's purse strings. When Ian moved to Jackson Hole, Wyoming, he lost that direct connection with his community, which some felt was a detriment to his health. In Utah, he was an integral part of the community (although he always kept a low profile in public). But in Jackson, he was just another wealthy tax fugitive.

Bob Hales used to say that Ian, despite being an atheist, "is one of the most spiritually sophisticated people that I know." Dad believed that religion offered a practical way of constructing ethics and morals that stimulated the best of human nature while constraining the worst human impulses. Religion established commonality and justified it through divinity. Ian was a worldly and enlightened thinker, but he didn't crave a spiritual practice for himself. He accepted that others needed it in their lives and felt that it was critical to maintaining the common good.

After spending time with our family friend, Mike Zimmerman, I got into Zen Buddhism. Dad asked me a lot of questions about it, and I regurgitated what I had learned in Zen 101, "to know the self, is to forget the self—reacting to every thought you have is a self-absorbed concept and meditation helps you to get over that." Dad decided to try it. He sat on a bench in the most tranquil spot he could think of for about four minutes. He scratched his scalp, gritted his teeth, and finally got up and proclaimed, "The problem with Buddhism is that it's narcissistic!" He was too ADHD to meditate, and he needed to justify his disinterest. So, in his typical, quick-witted, irreverent way, he highlighted the paradox of my chosen practice in one sentence, which irritated the hell out of me. The ultimate Grannyism! I said, "Don't Granny me on this subject right now!" He never meditated again, but he did understand and support that it was what I needed at the time.

Dad had a healthy respect for a higher power and would say things like "But for the grace of God go I" and "Keep a low profile or the Gods might get angry." He saw spirituality as the practice of checking one's ego and accepting one's place in the humanistic fiber of the world. This was an enigmatic stance because he was a card-carrying capitalist, but he was also a card-carrying humanist. He believed in karma but thought it was "a silly way to describe it." Ian thought that if we all lived by the Golden Rule (do unto others as you would have them do unto you), everyone's life would be better. Dad even tried to get HBS to teach classes to second-year students about the Golden Rule and its role in business. He believed that the objective measures of success—money, power, influence—had gotten out of balance. HBS was producing velociraptors, and what was needed was a more soulful, integrated form of business. His softer side believed that one style of leadership could not exist without the other and that in the United States, and maybe the world, we were on the wrong track. Dad's value system drove his ethics, his leadership style, and his philanthropic missions and he acted on the notion that we all have a responsibility to leave the world a better place than we found it with the resources available to us.

Damsels in Distress

Dad was a balanced and tolerant leader. He possessed a mind that could put deals together faster than a computer, and he was an intimidating negotiator and businessman. But he always had a weakness for the "Damsel in Distress," as my stepmother called them. I'm not sure if it was because these ladies were complete opposites to his mother, or maybe it was his altruism playing out in smaller ways outside the more formal world of philanthropy. I'm sure a psychiatrist would have a field day analyzing his motivations. Many women throughout his life—usually single moms, but not always—benefitted from his soft heart. How he made their acquaintance varied as much as their need: there was Sharon, who needed a new set of false teeth, and later Ian gave her a loan to start her own business; Cammy who needed gastro bypass surgery and some debt relief; Val who wasn't getting child support from her ex-husband, so Ian stepped up to help; Nikki who went to the Cleveland Clinic for her health problems on Ian's plane; Amy for whom he paid both college and medical school tuition; Megan whom he helped get into HBS, and the list goes on. They were all hard-working women who needed a little extra help. Ian's mother, Granny, told him, "The money is poison, and you are addicted to it, it's beneath you." My stepmother would often tell him that "the money doesn't count." The damsels had fallen on hard times, and he was empathetic to their situation. Helping them allowed him to feel like a provider and a benefactor. He was always faithful to Annette, but there was something about a woman in need that still appealed to his sense of power and innate generosity. As much as he supported equal rights for women and was attracted to strong women, he was born in 1940 so his view of gender roles was fairly traditional. I think that providing aid to these women fulfilled something in him; he created emotional support for himself by helping others.

Liberal Democratic Capitalist Pig

Dad held strong political beliefs, and he advocated for us to be intellectually plastic enough to hear and assimilate new information without being intimidated—in all walks of life.

When trying to bend the world to his will, he knew that politics was an inevitable part of the equation. Ian's theory, that every good capitalist system was balanced by a liberal democracy, informed his political affiliation as a liberal Democrat.

As Bud Scruggs said of Dad, "He respected the beliefs of others, but he was clear in rejecting their prejudices and he could disagree without anger." He would hear people out, but he had the self-assurance to not be threatened by their ideals. In today's political environment, people get vengeful if someone else has a different idea, just because it forces them to question their values. Ian wrote about politics in one of his shareholder letters, "Like children on the playground, no one gets their way all the time."

Dad supported candidates and initiatives that represented the duty he felt to advance the common good, and our family will continue to prioritize political involvement in the future.

Removing Himself from the Atmosphere

"As a young boy, growing up in Saskatchewan, I walked to school every day. I remember very cold mornings when my feet were freezing, and I yearned for spring. When spring came, I always associated it with the songs of the meadowlarks coming from the fields along my way. I always cherished this hopeful sound. When times are tough—or when we become consumed by the stress of our daily lives—I tell myself and my friends to 'remember the meadowlark.' It is a way I have of recalling my childhood, remaining hopeful and staying connected with nature."—Ian Cumming, The Nature Conservancy's Living Lands & Waters Campaign Celebration, 2009.

Nature, the outdoors, and being kind to the environment were always important to my father. When I was in high school Ian purchased a vacant lot in the Federal Heights neighborhood of SLC with a plan to build a house. Climate change was just starting to take shape in the mid-80s, and Ian was a data guy. He calculated his lung capacity and how many breaths he took per day and figured out how much carbon dioxide he would expel into the world throughout his lifetime. Then he determined how many trees it would take to offset his carbon dioxide impact on the environment. He planted that number of trees around the perimeter of the lot. I don't remember how many trees he planted, but it was a lot! He would chuckle as he told us that he had removed himself from the atmosphere. As a teenager, I thought it was an odd thing to do, but his analysis and commitment stuck with me.

His extended involvement and leadership in the Nature Conservancy of Utah are well documented and commemorated in a beautiful book that the team created in his honor. Ian liked to bellow, "We preserve nature the old-fashioned way, we buy it!" From an early age, he impressed upon us the importance of leaving the world better than how we found it. But he also emphasized that we all need to do the best we can in the scope of our own lives. While he worshipped at the altar of capitalism, he never stopped advocating for the common good, and he felt strongly that these two things do not have to conflict with one another. The economy drives the world stage in many ways, and often the most efficient and direct action is to exert influence as a consumer to foster change.

Anonymous in Public, Authentic in Person

Like the myth of the Raven bringing salmon to the river to feed the people, Dad firmly adhered to the concept of noblesse oblige. If we are fortunate enough to be able to improve our circumstances, we should extend a helping hand to others as well. He was equally emphatic about not seeking gratitude as a reward for doing the right thing, which is why most of his philanthropy was anonymous, and you won't see the Cumming name on any buildings. His motto, "Be anonymous in public and authentic in person" was most on display in this area of his life. The executive committee of one of the disease-related charities that Ian supported wanted to recognize his generosity by making him the honoree of their annual banquet.

Ian interrupted and asked, "How much did I give you for last year's dinner?" The response was $75,000. Ian replied, "I will give you a choice, you can leave here with another check for $75,000 or you can make me the honoree and I will never write another check." They left, happy with their check!

Dad believed that protecting the common good was paramount, even when that required "giving when it hurts the most." Philanthropy (sometimes recognized, but more often anonymous) has always been a focus for our family and will continue to be. Dad's philanthropic endeavors were usually thoughtful and controlled, but also sometimes verging on the impulsive (like the damsels in distress). In more simplistic terms, Dad made all the money, and he would give it away how he wanted to do it.

Art Appreciation

When Ian was a young man living in Kansas City, he was friendly with the daughter of artist Thomas Hart Benton, one of the most important artists in the United States at the time. Ian would get paid to help clean up his studio, and when he was done, he and Benton would share a glass of wine while they discussed art, and they struck up a friendship. This gave Ian an early window into having an association with a piece of art; he might not know the name of an artist, but he knew that he related to the content of the art in some way.

Ian's mother, Granny Elaine, had a creative side that complemented her scholarly pursuits. She loved to make intricate quilts with flowers that were constructed out of fabric with the Latin names of the flowers carefully embroidered on the bedspread. This art form allowed her to express her fondness for both botany and Latin; later in life, she gave these exquisite blankets as gifts to friends and family. I remember as a child drawing with watercolor pencils when we would visit her house.

Ian didn't inherit any of her artistic talents, but he did have an ingrained love of art and he helped pass that on to me and David. Back in the '90s, one of Dad's accountants suggested that he was not leveraged enough, and he needed more diversity in his portfolio. Consequently, he borrowed money and started investing in art. Collecting art with borrowed money was antithetical to his approach to life and capitalism, and it was contrary to everything he knew about investing. Despite that belief, with his usual vigor, he began educating himself about artists with the help of his friend and fellow Harvard alum, D. Dodge Thompson, who is the chief of exhibitions at the National Gallery of Art. According to Dodge, "Most masters of the universe just want to impress someone who visits their house, but that was not his goal. It meant something to him both morally and symbolically. His intellectual curiosity was being stimulated in an entirely new way." One of the paintings Ian procured was *The Flute Player*, painted by Thomas Hart Benton, which still hangs in our home at Snowbird. Ian also had a vast collection of Cowichan masks, sculptures, baskets, and totem poles that he loved to purchase as an homage to his birthplace and his upbringing in British Columbia.

At the time, to our unsophisticated way of thinking, it seemed extravagant and more like he was spending money instead of investing it. We were baffled by his apparent recklessness, but he would cock his head, shrug, and laugh it off, "One of these days, you will say, *He was a pretty smart old fart*." Of course, he was right, it was a sophisticated way to diversify his portfolio. While he truly enjoyed collecting and commissioning art, the other major benefit of art as a capital investment is that it can be discounted and is a convenient way to transfer wealth. As he got older, he asked David and me to go through the house and choose the pieces that we wanted. "It's beautiful, enjoy it during your lifetime!" he would encourage us. But we felt like tomb raiders, we weren't comfortable picking through his art while he was still alive. When he passed away, many of his pieces were worth ten to twenty times what he paid for them, making his art collection a significant portion of his estate.

During his lifetime, Ian commissioned over two dozen portrait paintings of important people in history including scientists, judges, religious and political figures, business moguls, musicians, and poets. Many of those paintings hang in The National Portrait Gallery so others can enjoy them. He felt it was part of his duty to promote and protect the common good by recognizing these historic figures and memorializing their contributions to society forever in a portrait. His philanthropy in this area also helped to further the careers of many portrait artists including Nelson Shanks, Chuck Close, Rob McCurdy, and Jack Beal. Ian commissioned *The Four Justices*, which for many years was the largest painting that hung in the National Portrait Gallery in Washington D.C. The massive painting represents some of the first women in history to be painted in a place of power. "The scale of the painting speaks to the grand accomplishments made by these four women and the example they set for future generations," the director of the museum noted.[5] In addition, Ian commissioned the portrait of I.M. Pei, a renowned Chinese American architect, painted by Richard Estes, and various photorealist portraits by Rob McCurdy including Nelson Mandela, The Dalai Lama, and Toni Morrison. He also loved southwest art and viewed it as a growth category and invested in several Maynard Dixon and LaConte Stewart paintings. Art ticked off many of the things on Ian's priority list—intellectual curiosity, solid financial investment, and promoting the common good—and it was something he could share with his family while he was alive, and after he was gone.

The Mischievous Raven

Dad was certainly a serious businessman, but what strikes me most as I look back is how playful he was with his family and friends. He was continually on the lookout for ways to have fun or get into mischief. With the help of some of his friends and assistants, I've included just a few of the abundant stories that made us laugh over the years.

Ian was a bit of a trickster, like the Raven, and enjoyed playing little

---

[5] Smithsonian, "Four Supreme Court Justices Featured in Grand-Scale Painting at the National Portrait Gallery," October 25, 2013, News Release, https://www.si.edu/newsdesk/releases/four-supreme-court-justices-featured-grand-scale-painting-national-portrait-gallery#:~:text=%E2%80%9CThe%20scale%20of%20this%20painting,women%2C%20about%20breaking%20barriers.%E2%80%9D

pranks on his friends. Bud Scruggs had a real sweet tooth, so occasionally when they were out for dinner, Ian would get ahold of the waiter and secretly instruct, "See that guy on the end, bring him one dessert first, and as he finishes it, start bringing him another until he has every dessert on the menu sitting in front of him."

Eventually, Bud would figure it out and the whole table would be in an uproar. He employed the same game when we were in college with some of my friends, replacing the desserts with beer. This didn't always produce the results he was looking for but was entertaining, nonetheless.

When we were young, David and I tried to teach Ian the made-up language of OP whereby you insert OP before every vowel sound. For example, horse would be hOPorse. Annie, Dad, David, and I were having dinner at the Cliff Lodge one night during one of our ski weekends, and the three of us could easily speak OP to each other, but Dad couldn't wrap his head around it. He made a full-on scene in the restaurant, as he asked the waiter, "Do you speak this ridiculous language?" When the waiter answered in OP, Dad proclaimed, "This is a conspiracy!" We tried to teach him using single-syllable words, so for every item he ordered, we encouraged him to order it in OP. His attempt to order a Coors Beer, which he loved at the time, would sound like COOPROPPERSOP, or a hamburger, would be HAMBUROPEROP. We would all wind up with stomachaches from laughing so hard.

David and I had many nicknames for our father over the years, but our favorite was "Wallet Pig" or just Wally for short. This was related to the fact that he referred to himself as a truffle pig, but also because he kept a billfold of crisp hundred-dollar bills with him at all times, usually about $4k-$5k worth. If a bill got crinkled or creased and didn't fit neatly into the stack, he would either give it to one of us kids or Annette. If family wasn't around, he would recycle them to someone in the office. He also had a pocket full of "littles"—twenties and under, reserved for smaller transactions. They didn't need to be quite as pristine as the hundreds but were neatly stowed all the same.

Dad's good friend Mike Zimmerman and his wife Lynne flew out to East Hampton to visit Ian with their two young children. Mike was a Justice on the Utah Supreme Court and a pretty intellectual guy, so he took great pride in the advancement of his children. Mike and Lynne were teaching their daughter to talk, doing the usual demonstration of items and repeating the word corresponding to that item. Ian, who loved being a jokester, would try to confuse her. Ian held up an apple to Alessa and said "Apple." Lynne joined in and reinforced the name, "Apple." Then Ian picked up a tennis ball and said, "Apple." Then he would pick up a fork and say, "Apple." He thought it great fun. A pouty look of confusion would cloud her face and Mike would get annoyed with Ian. From then on, the girls called him "Mr. Apple" and later when the family adopted a Lhasa Apso as a family pet, they named him Mr. Apple. They still joke about it to this day.

When Dad got a bit of money while working in SLC, he bought a big Kingsley camper, and he would sometimes take his buddies to southern Utah or Sun Valley for camping trips. Of the many legendary stories from those times, the one I remember most was a trip he took with a bunch of competitive alpha dog friends. One of the guys was being sanctimonious throughout the trip and was annoying everyone. On their way home, Ian pulled the large RV into the gas station in Snowville, and the irritating chap left the vehicle to use the restroom. Just as he was walking back toward the vehicle, Ian dramatically pulled away from the gas station stranding him there, and yelling out the window, "Don't worry, Peter, you will be mayor in a year!" They eventually came back to get him, but they all loved Ian's roguish side.

Ian always got very excited about food. Before a meal, he often looked like a hungry toddler waiting in his highchair. But he hated to contend with the "food police," which was probably either Annette or someone else elected to monitor his food intake. He would often work all day, and then head to the airport with his assistant, Wayne, to catch a flight for his next gig. On the way to the airport, he insisted on stopping at the Java Joe near the office where he ordered a Frozen Joe coffee drink. They drove slowly so he could savor every sip of that Frozen Joe on the way to the airport. No one likes to admit they go to fast food restaurants, and Ian was no different. Just as he would drive through the gate at the hangar, he would throw his Java Joe cup out the window so there was no evidence for the food police. When he got to the hangar, he told the staff, "I think someone is littering back there, you might want to clean it up!" Ian's impulses sometimes overtook his idealism.

At the family office, Ian's assistants would always order his lunch for him because he was either busy or didn't want to choose. He had three buttons on his desk telephone, and each button had its unique sound for the respective assistant. On one particular day, someone chose Mexican food for lunch. Soon after putting his lunch in front of him, all the bells went off steadily, which meant it was important. Two of his assistants quickly arrived in his office. Ian looked at them and said in a mock serious tone, "If you ever try to feed me a tortilla again, I will chop your peckers off."

Ian had gone to Zurich, Switzerland, to tour the R&D laboratory of a company that Leucadia was interested in. While there, he saw a strange-looking gun, and of course, his curiosity compelled him to ask what it was for. The tour guide informed him that one of the engineers had made it because he was looking for a safer "Potato Gun." A potato gun, also referred to as a potato cannon, or "spud gun," is a pipe-based cannon that uses air pressure to fire a projectile item, most often a potato or similarly textured food product. They took the gun out into the parking lot loaded an apple into it and shot the apple from the parking lot into an adjacent field. Ian had so much fun with it, that the engineer let him have it, assuring him that they could make more. Ian brought the gun to the family office with a huge grin on his face, he was so proud of that damn gun. One evening after work, a few people were lingering around the office, and Ian decided to pull out the potato gun. Mind you, the potato gun originated from the WWII-era Holman Projector, and in some states, it is illegal. Nevertheless, his trusty assistant Wayne, ran to the store to buy potatoes, which they proceeded to shoot off the east porch of the office on South Temple (affectionately and humorously referred to as The Mansion by family and staff). The odd piece of artillery sounded like a real shotgun, and as soon as they shot it off, Ian dropped the gun and sprinted his overweight body as fast as he could back into the mansion so he wouldn't get caught. Everyone present at the aborted military operation agreed it was the fastest they had ever seen him move.

No Such Thing as the Top

At some point when we were living in SLC and Dad had been working at a manic pace for years, he started to feel more self-assured in his success. He drove a fancy Mercedes, (which he referred to as "der Grosse," a reference to a German battleship), he was flying first class, etc. But he would look around at other businessmen who had private jets, drove Aston Martins, or had homes in the Hamptons, and he would mutter, "There is no such thing as the top." The process of accumulating capital continued to drive him; he was a junkie, addicted to the journey of making money and having more power. He was obsessed with the Brass Ring. Fundamentally he knew that he was at a point where his lifestyle wouldn't change if his net worth continued going up but, in his mind, there was no end, he was on a never-ending ladder, always looking at someone else's ass in front of him who seemed to have more than he did.

On the contrary, in mountain climbing, there is always a top. It is a contained, finite thing (although generally, someone's ass is still in front of you, at least you are on the same team). Sporting events nearly always have a start and a finish, winners, and losers, a score, and a time limit. This is why I gravitated towards sports and climbing in particular. I wanted the finiteness and the boundaries, as well as the ability to prove myself in a world where the contest was based on my skills and my speed—who *I* was, not who *my father* was. Watching my dad rarely achieve balance, and constantly live on this manic mission with no end had an impact on my choices. I wanted to be involved in things that I was passionate about and that I was proud of. I had a strong desire to be enterprising and successful, but I needed to do it on my terms.

Climbing the Pitch

The Mountain Climber

After attending grammar and some middle school in Utah, we were sent to boarding school for our remaining school years—David to St. George's in Rhode Island and me to the Kent School in Connecticut. We were fortunate that Dad could afford to send us to private school, and we played all the usual New England preppy sports, which we very much enjoyed, and we made friendships during our time at boarding school that have endured through the years.

At boarding school, my resentment of the capitalist ideals that took my father away from us continued to fester. His effort to attain and preserve capital felt like it came at the expense of time with his family. He had a couple of failed marriages, and we were raised by nannies. For me, this led to a complex relationship with my dad. Being an idealistic and immature teenager, I disavowed capitalism and everything it stood for. Despite my love for all the experiences and friends I had acquired on the East Coast, I always felt pulled to return to the mountains in the West. During my junior year at Kent, I was accepted to the University of Colorado Boulder, and my heart raced at the thought of returning to the mountains.

While Dad was a mad Canadian, I was a little edgier. I had abandonment issues with my mother, I was continually running from the fear of disappointing my father, and I headed off to UC Boulder with some pretty entrenched insecurities. I fell in with a group of rebellious kids and made an abundance of poor choices during my first two years at school. During the second semester of sophomore year, I stopped going to class and went skiing instead. A bumper sticker on my jeep read, "Ski Now, CU later." I was too stupid and distracted to withdraw, so I flunked out.

"I'm not paying for you to be a ne'er-do-well! Get your head out of your ass! You are cut off!" Dad informed me.

Despite our traumatic experience on the Grand Teton, we continued to climb on glaciated peaks as a family throughout our teenage years (not rock climbing like at the Tetons), and I found that I enjoyed it and had some natural ability at altitude. The summer before I started college, we had traversed the Alps via La Haute Route from Chamonix to Saas-Fee with Peter Whittaker, a world-famous veteran climbing guide who comes from a long line of accomplished mountaineers. Pete ended up having to hire some French speakers to help with the climb because none of us spoke French. I learned two things during this route: I liked Pete, and I wanted to learn French.

When I flunked out of Boulder, I moved to Mount Rainier to train to become a climbing guide with Lou Whittaker, thanks to an introduction from Pete. Between climbing seasons, I traveled to Paris to learn French (Dad would always pay for school if we were performing academically). Climbing gave me a focus that I desperately needed. It made me get my act together, offered me the challenge of mastering a skill, and I was attracted to the community that climbing provided. I was able to move up and down the mountain quickly, I could carry heavy loads and I was a good communicator. Because of my earlier experience with Ted Wilson on the Tetons, I was empathetic to new climbers. I enjoyed the responsibility of leading others and the comfort of being part of a team. In the climbing fraternity, I found the family I craved.

Climbing recentered my life and gave me something to care about. While we celebrated often, partying was no longer the priority in my world. Every time I touched the summit of Mount Rainer (a total of sixty-nine times—the last time was with my wife, Kristi), a part of that awful experience on the Grand was exorcised from my brain. The failure in the Tetons had haunted me for the previous decade, but I had finally figured out a way to recraft it in my own light. After seven years of climbing and attending college when I could, I became a senior guide and finally graduated with a degree in French from CU. Interestingly, one of the things I learned as a guide is that we were NEVER allowed to take kids under the age of 14 climbing. PERIOD. They don't have the clarity of thought or perspective to think beyond their discomfort at the present moment. As I had experienced firsthand, they can only feel pain, fatigue, and cold. They can't anticipate the satisfaction they will have upon completing such a difficult feat. It made me realize that Dad probably persuaded Ted to take me on that climb and that in reality, I had not failed, I had survived.

The years when I was climbing provided the best leadership, management, team building, and communication training I would ever receive, and it was within an ecosystem that resonated with me. We approached every climb as a new entrepreneurial venture—each one different but always with a great deal of uncertainty to be navigated. I learned how to synthesize information and make decisions under pressure. Weather patterns and topographical changes presented external challenges over which I had no control but had to mitigate. I became proficient in crafting a concise message and relaying it to the team. I worked to build trust with each team member, so they had faith in me as their leader. I relished the success of a magical summit with everyone on the expedition when things went right but took responsibility when things went wrong. Ian had received his education at HBS and Turner Uni-Drive, and I received mine on the mountain. When my father saw Lou a few years later at Snowbird he said, "I sent you a boy, and you sent me a man."

"If You Could Fall Out of a Sleeping Bag, I Would Have" (The Birth of Mountain Hardware)

One day, Dad called me out of the blue and said, "I want you to guide me up Denali." At first, I was incredulous—here was this fifty-three-year-old self-described "portly business executive" who lived in three-piece suits, flew private jets, and did not exercise asking me to guide him up Denali. Denali, also known as Mount McKinley, is the highest mountain peak in North America with a summit elevation of 20,310 feet. The trip would take around three weeks, and I had my doubts about whether he was up to the task, but he was asking to come into my world, so I recruited my two oldest and most competent climbing friends, Robert Link and Win Whittaker, to help us. We called ourselves the strong-back, small-brain team.

As we embarked that spring of 1992, we were slow and the guides (Ian not so much) carried monster loads, but as with everything in his life, Ian was emphatically resolved and determined to succeed. Through pure force of will, the junkyard dog slowly hauled his out-of-shape butt to the summit. Summit day was beautiful, and as we sat for a rest before the long descent, Ian was slumped over with duct tape on his nose to block the sun (like all good Canadians), eating elk jerky and guzzling water. He announced to the group, "No matter what I thought of myself when I started, I sit before you a tired, fat, old man." He had been humbled by the experience whereas I felt euphoric. This climb represented such deep closure for me; I had gotten my dad up the highest mountain in North America, and the purging of the Grand Teton debacle was complete for both of us. But the summit represented even more than that. Dad had reached out to me and showed faith in me, and that fact meant everything. He entered my domain, and in doing so, he was able to witness the skills I had developed and honed. I had assembled the right team, synthesized information, communicated effectively, and made critical decisions as a leader, in an environment that I valued. I felt his affirmation, and he felt mine. I felt his appreciation, and he felt mine. It was the convergence of mutual respect between father and son.

Ian was always motivated by food, and one of the mountain treats that we prepared was pies. We used store-bought pie tins and crusts, added pudding mix, and let it freeze overnight. The next day we would dangle the treat in front of him as a reward for enduring another part of the journey. I will never forget the image of my father sitting in the snow cave with his yellow down jacket and down booties scarfing down the remainder of the pie crust at the end of the day. He banged it on the ground to loosen the frozen crust and then licked the tin when he was done. The lightness and high spirit of that moment differed sharply from the dark austerity of his office and his corporate job. The demands of his career seemed far away from us at that moment.

Denali often has storms, and this trip was no different. Dad and I ended up stuck in a tent, huddled together for about four days. We were closer during this time than we had been for years, and were enjoying each other's company tremendously, or as much as you can in a small space. Dad snored like a freight train, and the altitude only made it worse. Finally, I had enough. As the condensation built, rime ice crystals accumulated in the top of the tent. I reached up and pulled one of the strings that were drying our socks and then scuttled back under my sleeping bag as the ice hit him in the face. He sat bolt upright, looked around, mumbled WTF, and then went back to his noisy slumber.

Four days is a long time to be alone together, and in addition to some frustrating and humorous experiences, we also had many heartfelt conversations. At one point, Dad told me, "I'm proud of you, son. Good for you for following your dreams. I admire the commitment that you have to the outdoor industry and healthy lifestyle and for not following me into my crazy world." He was complimentary, accepting, and loving. In his voice, I heard the pride that I had always longed for, and a satisfied grin crept over my face.

I uttered my gratitude and then said something along the lines of, "Actually, yeah, about that… the whole climbing thing is cool, but I'm kind of sick of being broke and eating ramen daily and I thought that maybe you could help me figure out how to be enterprising but still be involved in the outdoors?"

Dad would later express his feeling of shock at my request, "If you could fall out of a sleeping bag, I would have." We continued to discuss the possibility of combining his love for entrepreneurship with my love for the outdoors. I explained that the North Face uniforms we received every year didn't work and that they were inadequate for the conditions we dealt with. The guides dutifully provided useful details on the feedback form that North Face sent us: the jackets were hydrophilic, so we got wet; the waist belt of the pack dug into the drawstring at the waist, so we got bruised; and the sleeves were too long and didn't ventilate; etc. And the following year, we would get the same equipment back with no improvements.

"Dad, I think that this is an area where I could initiate change or maybe we could figure out something to do in the outdoor clothing or equipment business," I said.

"I would love to help you do that, go find a deal!" he responded wholeheartedly. I honestly didn't know what he meant by that, but I was ready to set off on a mission.

But first, we had to get safely off the mountain after the storm. As I learned time and again, the most technical and dangerous part of any climb is the descent. We had already come off the summit and spent the night at high camp at 17,000 feet and were heading further down to the advanced camp at 14,000 feet of elevation via the West Buttress route, which is one of the most stunning routes on Denali. Everyone was exhausted, especially my father. This is the crux of the climb; the conditions are extreme. It is 1000 feet of steep, bordering on 100% vertical ice, so fixed lines are a necessity because the belay rope going between the team is not enough. Fixed lines are anchored into this part of the mountain to protect climbing teams from falls that could be injurious or even fatal. To clarify, during this part of the climb there was the belay line that was holding the team together, and there was also the fixed line that we had to navigate with multiple carabiners (with webbing) being clipped and unclipped as we passed over each anchor while managing the ice axes and crampons that we had been using over the last three weeks. Then we came to the bergschrund, which is a type of crevasse that is formed when the ice pulls away from the rock. As descents go, it doesn't get much more difficult. It is also at this point, where you can see the camp at 14,000 feet just below and the view, when you can take a moment to look up from the multitude of lines and equipment, is surreal.

We were roped up together, moving slowly, in unison so as not to create too much tension or slack in the line, as we maneuvered through the pitch and crevasse. It was complicated, but also the safest way to descend that section. Each of us paused as we moved our carabiners over the anchors, and again as we navigated the bergschrund. If you are an experienced climber, you know where to put your crampons for success and can jump over the crevasse. Dad tried to jump too, but he was too fatigued and fell victim to a common, but dangerous, mountaineering mistake which we dubbed "the twelve-point crossover." While he was trying to cross the bergschrund, the toe of his crampon caught the heel of his other crampon. If he had been standing on the ground when this happened, he would have immediately face-planted, but since he was on a rope, he fell headfirst into the crevasse. I immediately self-arrested and was able to stop his fall and my own. As I looked down between my legs, I could see all 250 pounds of him dangling below me on his harness, legs in the air, laughing like the rascally Raven! He had hired a strong, competent team to safely guide him up AND down the mountain, and deal with situations exactly like the one he was in. I believe his laughter was a nervous reaction—he knew that he had messed up, but it also was kind of funny to see his large form dangling from the rope face first. I'm not sure if he was aware of how close he had come to not only killing himself but the entire team at that moment. I managed to hoist him up, which contributed to a chronic back injury that I still feel today. While I was bruised and battered when we got to camp, I was grateful that I was able to save his life and that he hadn't been injured.

As soon as I got home, I convinced one of the super senior guides, Joe Horiskey, who was responsible for scheduling, to let me go to the Reno Outdoor Retailer show. I showed up at the Outdoor Retailer show—an emaciated climber dude with sunburned raccoon eyes—and I proceeded to have a bunch of cocktails with an old friend named Skip Yowell with whom I had climbed Mount Rainier several times. I sat on the edge of my chair yakking this guy's ear off, throwing my hands around and describing my ideas. Skip was one of the founders of Jansport, and he knew everyone in the climbing world. He told me that there was some turmoil going on in the industry and a lot of companies were for sale, including Moonstone, North Face, and Sierra Designs. Having finally tired of my overzealous questions, he placated me. "I'll introduce you to my friend Jack Gilbert. He played basketball at Stanford. He's like six foot eight inches tall, big bushy mustache, he has been in the industry forever. He's not a climber; he's a businessman, and he is trying to put a group together to buy Sierra Designs."

True to his word, he set up an appointment for me to meet Jack the next day. The contrast of this super tall, bigger-than-life confident basketball player turned businessman with this skinny climber who had virtually no business experience, but an abundance of enthusiasm must have been quite a thing to see. I excitedly told him about my ideas, admitted to not having any practical business knowledge, and offered up my dad as the deal maker to persuade him to take me seriously. Although somewhat dubious of me at first, Jack decided to meet with Dad and me. We examined several companies over the next few months, but they either had a lot of problems that would have been too time-consuming and expensive to fix or were just plain not affordable for us to acquire.

Ultimately, we decided to start fresh and create our brand, unconstrained by poor product quality, supply, or distribution issues. And that is when Mountain Hardware was born. We could never quite remember who first said it, but I credit Dad with saying, "Why don't we just start from scratch?!" Jack was the leader and the brand guy, and we recruited Paul Kramer to be the brains of the operation and help us figure out how to design, source, and build great products. Paul and Jack had operational control, and Dad, David, and I had financial control. I also helped recruit some of the great climbers to promote our gear, including my good friend Ed Viesturs, who was on his way to climbing all fourteen of the 8,000-meter peaks. Ed provided his expert design ideas based on real-world alpine experience. He gave the brand a lot of visibility, and in turn, he got some money to fund his expeditions. It was a win-win at the time, and he became even more involved with the brand as it grew.

One of the many chips I had on my shoulder at the time was that whatever I did, I knew I would always be thought of as the descendant of a wealthy Wall Street guy. In general, we humans are overloaded with information, so to make sense of things in our brains, we categorize people within the construct of our own experiences. Even though most people get help from someone in their career, lots of folks categorized me as the recipient of a silver spoon. This perception occasionally worked to my advantage; people would underestimate me, and I would use that camouflage to eventually disarm them in ways they did not anticipate.

As I found my way back into the fold and asked for Dad's mentoring and support, he was happy to give it. But as we put together the deal (mostly designed by Dad because this was his forte and his fortune), he included a loan at the market rate.

I asked, "Are you really going to charge me 10% interest?"

He replied as only a pragmatic capitalist with integrity could, "Number 1—I expect a risk-adjusted return on my capital, number 2—you aren't going to find anything cheaper, and number 3—when you pay me back, you will be able to look in the mirror and know that regardless of what anyone else says, you did it." He structured our contract in a manner that would allow me to pursue business on my terms while honoring the realities of capitalism. In doing so, I could be satisfied with my accomplishments.

The team put their heads down to focus on creating a high-quality, dependable brand of technical gear. Within ten years we had accomplished that goal, and other outdoor companies were looking to acquire us. Dad had structured the deal so that our family would be in charge of any decisions related to selling the business. As perpetuity investors, Ian, David, and I didn't really want to sell, and objectively speaking, it probably would have made sense to hang on to the company and continue to grow it. But as I looked at the subjective facets of the situation, the context didn't feel right to me. I recognized that the majority of the people who had worked with us over the last ten years had also previously been involved in other ventures without a payout.

They had busted their butts to create an unbelievable brand and a profitable company, and this was their summit day.

I told Ian, "Columbia is a good company, Mountain Hardware will be in good hands, everyone is going to make money, and it is time for our team loyalty to outweigh our financial best interests." He was not happy with me, but it was my deal as it related to the family, so he deferred to me. My dreams were somewhat crushed because I wanted us to be the next Patagonia, but I put aside avarice and selfishness and did what I thought was best for the group. And we did all make money; I was fortunate to be able to build our family home in Park City with the profit we made from the sale, and it was my first big score.

The Kautz Crevasse

The Kautz is a classic climb up Mount Rainier. It is a hanging glacier on the south side of the mountain, and it was by far my favorite route to guide; the exposure was thrilling, and the views were stunning. Since it's more technical, it's less frequently climbed. The climbers gain altitude quickly. Several steep and exposed areas of terrain, dangerous crevasses, areas of rock fall, avalanches, and ice fall are not uncommon along this route. To me, it was the most satisfying route on Mt. Rainer, because the risk was high and the reward more savory. As a climbing team tackling the Kautz, our decision processes had to be better, and our reliance on each other was imperative. Step, breathe, plant the ice axe, and flip the rope. Over and over like a metronome. The acute angles of light and the sound echoing off the walls of the chute in the darkness under headlamps made it a meditative experience.

We were lucky enough to see an alpenglow as the sun rose during our ascent that morning. One of the most beautiful things you will ever see during a climb is the alpenglow. The sun's reflected light creates a reddish glow on the mountain when the solar disk is just below the horizon. This optical phenomenon does not happen often, but when it does—usually just before sunrise or sunset—it is otherworldly in its beauty. We were also fortunate to have a gorgeous summit as well.

As we began our descent, I was the "tail gunner." Dave Hahn (who is now a world-renowned alpinist) was leading the team; we had three in the middle, and I was in the back. It was a perfect day for climbing, and we had taken our time getting to the summit. As we made our way down (which is usually the sketchiest part), Dave was leading out and uncoiling the rope as we traversed a rock section and headed back onto the snow. Suddenly, an ice bridge that he didn't see collapsed under him, and he disappeared head-first into a hole about 40 or 50 feet down a deep crevasse. We hadn't fully uncoiled, so there was slack in the rope causing his fall to pull the clients between us off their feet and towards the hole through which he had disappeared. The hissing noise of the accelerating rope was terrifying, and as a tail gunner, I knew I didn't have much time to make the right decision. Since I was still on the rock, I couldn't self-arrest, so I decided to run down the hill and wrap the rope off on a large, seemingly stable rock—it seemed to work.

Once those of us aboveground were secure, we started a crevasse rescue procedure. Although Dave was a little beat up, he had managed to right himself and started to use his ascenders to climb back up the rope towards the surface. Ultimately, he appeared under his power, slightly bloodied, and bruised, but mostly pissed that he lost his guide hat somewhere in the depths of the glacier. Dave was a strong climber, we had a really good team, and we had all reacted in the ways we were supposed to, so we averted a disaster. But it was an extremely impactful moment for me and reminded me of when I had to save my father on Denali. The amazing, glorious summit day on my favorite route with a strong and competent experienced team was a stark contrast to the fact that a major incident had still occurred. It was the solidification in my brain of the lessons of climbing and how they relate to life. Even when you are prepared and well-supported, awful things can surprise you. But if you have the right tools, whether climbing tools, healthcare tools, or business tools—they need to be sharp, and you need to know how to use them.

Every Step Up Is Optional

The lessons I learned as a guide helped me gain confidence and resilience and made me a more understanding human being, and ultimately, a better businessperson. What started as a rebellious gesture turned into a guiding principle for my business and my life.

In alpine mountaineering, in preparation for an expedition, teams are picked, a route is mapped out, and camps are established at different elevations (called islands of safety). Supplies are ferried to the various camps so the climbers can stage through on their way to the summit. The team climbs together for days or weeks under heavy loads in ever-increasing exposure, altitude, and cold—amidst the constant danger of avalanches and rock falls. Summit Day represents the culmination of planning, provisioning, logistics, and work done by many people. It is always a long and by far the most difficult day because so much time and energy has already been consumed. When the window of opportunity presents itself (a clear forecast) the summit bid is planned.

Most often in an alpine ascent, we depart the high camp in the wee hours of the morning, around 3:00 a.m. Every climber is tied to another for protection, so if anyone missteps the others are there to catch him. Freezing night-time temperatures make the mountain safer, binding rock, ice, and snow together in a more solid state. Each climber is focused inward toward the mountain, brows furrowed in concentration, moving in a disc of light from the headlamp that spans no more than six feet in front of them. Within that narrow focus and the contours of the frozen snow, each climber searches for the right place for the crampon and ice axe, resulting in tiny robotic steps that go on for hours. Breathe. Chunk. Step. Breathe. Chunk. Step. On constant repeat. The team moves slowly and methodically, tethered together as a rope team. In the narrow beam of light through the black night, we have one thought on our minds—the anticipation of making it to the summit. Every small, repetitive step is making progress toward that goal.

The sun comes up during the last couple hours of the ascent, and when we finally reach the top, we are met with an intoxicating view. The team has taken millions of steps to get to this point and has been uncomfortable for days and weeks at a time. We give each other hugs and celebrate for a moment or two, take the hero shots and refuel. We are proud of what we accomplished, but we know three things: it doesn't count unless we get home, we are less than half done, and 75% of falls occur on the way down. The goal is to drive by the mountain adoringly afterward, not to be part of the mountain for the rest of eternity. Consequently, not much time is spent on the summit before we begin the descent.

The myopic, glacial, solid, conditions that typified the ascent have changed; the earth underfoot is slippery because the mountain has heated up, balance is challenged, avalanche risk and rock fall danger are exponentially higher, and the exposure field is seemingly infinite—we gaze outward instead of inward. No matter how experienced the climber is, everyone has expended most of their emotional and physical energy getting to the summit. Our hearts are pounding, and our breath is thick, and now is the time when we need to be thinking the most clearly. We need to readjust our focus and execution and make good decisions because we still have several days of walking before we are safe again.

This is when the work truly begins, and all the passion seems like it was left on that summit; at the moment when we are the least well equipped, our brains and our bodies need to be at their sharpest. As guides, we must motivate our emotionally and physically exhausted team to safely descend the mountain. It requires patience, clear communication, trust, and the higher goal of living to climb another day.

Just as my father had his rules for investing, I live by the rules I learned during climbing expeditions:

- Every step up is optional, but each step down is mandatory; the goal is to climb another day
- When you encounter a sketchy part of the mountain, go as light as you can—don't add rocks to your pack
- You can't always pick your summit day
- Climb the mountain one pitch at a time
- Hope for the best and prepare for the worst
- We go through life with heavy loads and light loads, adapt as needed
- If you are not adding strength to the team, or worse, creating risk for the group, you may be asked to stay at high camp or leave the climb altogether
- Sometimes around sunset, if the light is just right, you can see the shadow of the mountain that you are climbing in the atmosphere. It is beautiful, stop to appreciate it.

Learning to Spell

We had a family tradition of getting together sometime in November to buy all of our ski equipment at Kindersport in Park City. This started years before we ever got involved in the ski industry, and we continued the tradition of getting our gear in Park City (although not at Kindersport) even as we got older. During the fall of 1992, the whole family was on Main Street in Park City—me, David, Annette, and Ian. I had my degree from CU Boulder, was an advanced climber, and we had started Mountain Hardware. I was passionate about the brand and offered input where it was needed, but it was not a full-time gig for me. Dad was probing me about my plans, and honestly, I was uptight about what I was going to do next. I wanted to be affirmed as a "serious person" to my father; his love was the most important currency in my life. But at that point, I just knew that I didn't want to do what he did. Everything about the mountains resonated with me: the sweet smell of the pine trees, the snow puffs gathering on the branches, the noise of the wind blowing over the mountain, and the rush of flying over a cornice. The whole environment created a sort of homing pigeon instinct within my soul. As we walked out of the restaurant, a clean autumn aroma was blowing down Main Street. That crisp mixture of sweet and sour, old and new, and the changing of the seasons energized me.

"Whatever it is that I do," I declared. "I want to be able to smell this pure mountain smell every day!"

"Then go do it!" Dad replied, just as supportive as he had been previously. "I will help you."

Dad had seen firsthand my passion for the mountain industry through my climbing and involvement with Mountain Hardware, and he wanted to test me a bit more before making any further investments in me. He started working through his connections to find more opportunities for me to demonstrate my commitment to the business. His first call was to Gordon Strachan. Gordon was an unindicted co-conspirator in the Watergate mess under Nixon, but all charges against him were dropped. He decided he needed to exit that scene quickly and moved to Utah in 1975 to be a lawyer in the ski industry. Through various channels, Ian and Gordon had become good friends, even though they were on opposite sides of the political spectrum. They bonded over the difficulty of raising sons, among other things. Their wives were friendly, our families took several trips together over the years, and Ian and Gordon ultimately served on the 2002 Olympic

Committee together. Gordon knew Nick Badami, the owner of Park City Resort at that time, from his time in the ski world. Gordon also knew that Nick had recently lost his only son, Craig, in a tragic helicopter crash in 1989 during America's Opening at the Women's World Cup hosted by Park City Mountain Resort (PCMR).

Gordon was quick to figure out that perhaps a union between me and my family and Nick and his family could be mutually beneficial—I could learn about the ski industry firsthand under his tutelage, and Nick would appreciate having a mentee to pass on his vast knowledge to. Gordon worked his magic and convinced Nick to meet with me. My visit to meet Nick was my very first business trip, and I remember it clearly. I showed up in San Francisco and called Nick, and he told me to meet him at the Fairmont Hotel. I cleared my throat nervously and responded, "I don't know where that is, but I'll try to find it." What a jughead, I should have just said, "Yes Sir." I made my way there and was thoroughly intimidated by Nick, who had piercing, dark eyes, and a thick mane of white hair. Nevertheless, I eagerly blabbed to him about the mountain smell, my love of climbing, and combining business with being outside—my whole schtick. Nick told me about an avalanche that had taken place at Alpine Meadows (one of his ski resorts) and how he appreciated climbers because they were the only group who were clear minded during the stress of that catastrophe. Despite my obvious inexperience, he reasoned that I must have some skill and ability because of my success as a guide. At the very least, he knew I had the perseverance to carry heavy packs uphill for long periods day after day, which is exactly what the ski industry demands at times. Nick was pretty old school and had that "drop the kid in the deep end and see if he surfaces" mentality, so he created a management training program for me.

At the time, the whole resort team was still reeling from the wound left by Craig's sudden death. Craig had striking charisma, and although

I never met him, I felt his presence every day that I spent at the resort. For the next year, I was the only management trainee at PCMR. Nick would parachute me into each department, and they would begrudgingly train me on the task at hand. I started off working in the race department, which was physically demanding and tiring. When I mastered one department, I would be shuttled to the next. I continued onto reservations, where everything was done on paper and over the phone at the time, which was archaic, time-consuming, and required mountains of patience. I was the only male and the only employee under the age of thirty in the room. As you can imagine, they were not keen on having some kid from the CEO's office drop into their environment, and they looked at me with their arms crossed over their chest. I had to disarm them with my work ethic, reliability, and good nature. They enjoyed pointing out my inadequacies, and I just kept working and learning with a smile plastered on my face. I moved on to lift operations, World Cup race prep, grooming, ski school, and snowmaking. Like climbing mountains, I learned the ski business one step at a time, and as my dad demanded, I was walking the factory floor.

Throughout my training, Nick watched me and talked to my supervisors as he moved me around the many departments of the resort. At the same time, Dad was also watching—to determine whether I had the dedication and pain tolerance to succeed in the industry. Nick was testing, monitoring, and measuring me against the backdrop of his misery and the loss of his son. I will be forever grateful to Nick for taking me under his wing during such a vulnerable time in his life. All the while, Craig's huge legacy stood over me. I was constantly judging myself against the ideal that I had created in my mind of Craig Badami. That pressure helped me to become the very best version of myself that I could imagine at the time. During this important mentoring period, I was able to prove to both my father and Nick my absolute dedication to the craft of management. I was a serious person and I had conviction, both of which were gold in the eyes of my father.

It was 1994, and Nick had owned the company for twenty years. He didn't appreciate the rampant conglomeration going on in the business. He was keen on maintaining the community feel of the mountain and keeping PCMR family owned. Intrawest was angling to make PCMR a strategic part of its business holdings, but Nick wanted to maintain the family-friendly resort he had nurtured from its infancy. Soon after my anniversary of training at Park City, Dad called and asked me to meet him to discuss a few things.

Ian said, "Nick was here. He wants to sell his company, and he wants us to buy it, and he will teach you how to run it. But I think it is too early. You should go to business school."

I replied, "You can't always pick your summit day." I had found the answer to what I wanted to do when I grew up.

At that point in my life, I knew almost nothing about business and even less about what is involved in a merger. I watched in amazement as Nick and Dad managed lawyers, negotiated with banks, and seemed to communicate telepathically during the whole process. In many situations with a wealthy father, the patriarch will usually fund the child and let him go off on his own. The fact that Ian made it a priority to maintain and foster our connection and to show me the ropes along the way is a testament to the dedication he had to his family. I was able to learn from two superstars in their respective industries; no business school education could match the remarkable mentoring that fate brought my way.

Finally, we got the deal done and flew to the Bank of Boston for the closing. We were in one of those big rooms with a ridiculously long conference table with twenty chairs around it and stacks and stacks of paperwork that needed to be signed. We all played musical chairs as we moved through the paperwork. Ironically, I was surrounded by people in suits in a stuffy professional office building with absolutely no mountain smell! Before we could complete the sale, the lawyers notified us that we needed a name for our company. My eyes widened, and I looked around in panic, I didn't have a name or any ideas. I looked to my mentor, Nick, and said, "What should we call it?" After a brief pause, he said, "How about POWDR without the E?"

"Sure," I said, "Why?"

"Because it was on Craig's license plate when he died."

That gesture, so grand and yet so subtle, was the final validation of the training I had received. It put a resounding exclamation point on both of our intents. He didn't need to say anything more; at that moment I was unspeakably honored and grateful to be chosen to uphold the legacy of the Badami family and their commitment to mountain life. We strive to honor this legacy every day at POWDR in the way we thoughtfully create our portfolio of mountain experiences, manage our resorts, and treat our employees and customers.

My Part, Your Part

"Love Your Friends, Discard Your Enemies, Tell the Truth, and Keep your Contracts" [Hate your enemies is what he actually said, but the family has amended this "Ianism" because hate seemed too harsh!]

This was probably the motto that my father is most well-known for among his friends and family, as both my brother and Bud Scruggs reminded me. As I reflect on all of the things that Ian taught me, this story is one of my favorites and nicely encapsulates Dad's principles and the impact of his legacy on my life. The shorter version of this axiom that Dad taught us when we were young children was "My Part, Your Part." Dad explained that if you live life in this manner—tell the truth, love your family, be a good citizen, and keep your contracts— then you are "doing your part." When David and I were younger that meant getting good grades, doing our chores, etc. It was a model, not just for business, but also for how to conduct our lives.

After my management training program at PCMR, which served as "walking the company floor" and made sure I would "never invest in a business that I didn't fully understand," Dad knew I was serious about my entrepreneurial mission. Dad loaned me money at market interest rates to start POWDR, with all of the covenants similar to a bank loan—not to mention the "psychic interest" of borrowing money from my father[6]. I would have picked death over failure to repay any loan I took from him. The conditions of my jumping into the business world were that I had to abide by the rules of capitalism, and I had to play full contact like everyone else. In fact, maybe I had to play faster and harder than others to overcome the stigma of nepotism. We can be a family and we can be in business together, but all of the principles of business and capitalism still apply. Ian's capital got us started, but Ian allowed Nick to mentor me in ways that he knew he could not as my father. Ian allowed Nick to lead, and me to follow, and he got out of the way. Dad knew that the father-son relationship was to be preserved at all costs, so he always used a mentor intermediary. In retrospect, I see that I couldn't have done it *with* him, but I couldn't have done it *without* him either. It was a balance that we actively navigated.

Building a company in a non-growth industry characterized by volatility takes a combination of pugnacious tenacity, high pain tolerance, creative thinking, and a lot of luck. Nick and Dad were there, always taking my calls, giving advice as requested, and offering coaching and love. Dad kept me centered and gave me confidence in my own instincts and decision-making abilities. Once again, Dad encouraged me to leap while he stayed loyally by my side, just like our ski adventures at Snowbird. All the while, he was watching and assessing me to determine

---

[6] Ian loaned the money to POWDR which was owned by David and me. David was in college at the time and didn't join the business until later. Dad never played favorites!

whether I had what it took to be a business leader.

Several years later, I invited Dad to take a stroll on the beach with me as we often did on vacation in East Hampton. We walked by the hedges that hid the WASPy east coast mansions on Ocean Avenue, entered the public beach via the usual route that I had taken every year since I was a teenager, and complained about the distance. Our conversation paused for a bit as we listened to the powerful waves crashing onto the sand. The Hamptons held a special place in both of our hearts. Dad felt that he had finally made it when he was able to buy a house there, and I had many fond memories of running around with a pack of teenagers in my youth. He didn't know that as we walked, I had a check in my pocket that I wadded up and clenched nervously. In the middle of our coastal trek between Main Beach and Georgica Beach, in the early morning seaside light, I said, "Oh by the way, I almost forgot to give you this," and I handed him the crumpled check, which represented the payoff of all the money I had borrowed with interest. "I love you and thank you," I added. He opened the check, looked up at the sky, fell back into the dunes, and started crying. He did his part and loaned me money, and I did my part—I paid him back. It was a specific contract with my father about money, but also a greater symbolic contract about the way we work—we keep our contracts with the world but most of all with one another. I upheld our commitment, and I was living by the honor code that my father had established. The mountain climber with a chip on his shoulder had graduated to serious ski industry operator.

Rocket Boosters

Everyone needs strong rocket boosters to help them along their journey. These are people or groups of people whose efforts or intentions drive you forward. They help you break through the gravitational forces in the atmosphere to experience a boost. But like a rocket, at some point, they need to drop off and the timing of the boosting and falling away is critical. Sometimes during our life, we need rocket boosters, and at other times, we become a rocket booster for others. I was fortunate to have several crazy-smart, experienced rocket boosters during my career. Ian obviously was one, Nick Badami was another, and there have been many other mentors along the way. Their experience, resolve, perspective, and counsel made them some of the best rocket boosters anyone could have, and then they fell away and let me continue my path.

Nick was an incredibly effective booster during my training at PCMR, but there was a point where I knew it was time for his booster to fall away from the rocket. This happens for a variety of reasons. Some need to lighten the load to get into orbit or the rocket must change its trajectory to get to the desired destination or maybe the atmosphere has changed, and they need different tools to navigate. When it was time for Nick to retire, the construct in my mind was that we were transitioning into orbit, and it was time to drop the booster. I thought it was an important conversation to have in person, especially because of all Nick had done for me. I flew to Tucson where he was living with his wife and told him I thought it was time for me to take over as CEO and he could be chair of the board.

Nick responded, "How much did you spend to fly down here? You could have called me. I thought you were going to do this months ago." I was dumbfounded and speechless and loved him all the more.

What I discovered not long after is that it's scary and lonely when you are in orbit. Losing all that support and stability was more challenging than I anticipated. I thought I could run things at PCMR by myself, but I quickly figured out that was a mistake. I didn't have as much experience as I needed to lead a large company, and I made a lot of errors. We did some great things, but we also went backward in some ways. I needed a pro, and Vern Greco was a bona fide, seasoned executive who launched me to the next level of strategic business decision-making. During the 2001 downturn, we had the dot com bust, the Olympics were coming to Utah, and several things needed to be strategically addressed. Unfortunately, we had to reduce our overhead, which meant cutting down full-time equivalent employees and some seasonal staff. We had many philosophical discussions about where those lines could and should be drawn. We analyzed what was a franchise and what was a service. We established KPIs (key performance indicators) and benchmarked each department. We measured objective and subjective criteria over time, which allowed us to make informed decisions that would support both enduring and shorter-term goals. Vern taught me so much about the business, organization, and the value of the rocket booster throughout life.

Kristi

In addition to a career path that I was passionate about, one of the most important things that PCMR brought into my life is my wife, Kristi Terzian Cumming. Kristi was a superstar ski racer on the World Cup for many years and only missed going to the Olympics because of a knee injury. Just after POWDR purchased PCMR, Kristi owned a coffee shop at the resort and was also the ski ambassador for PCMR. I was a huge fan of hers but had not yet met her, and I was already engaged to another woman. My father had a group of buddies that included Dick Marriott (of the hotel chain), Gordon Strachan, and Nick Badami. We would all occasionally go on ski trips together. In the winter of 1995, I met Dick in Vancouver to go on a heli-skiing trip as part of the group. He and I were driving up to Whistler together, and I was a bit intimidated by Dick. He was a heavy hitter in the corporate world, and I was just starting. About halfway into our drive, he said to me,

"Your counsel of mentors asked me to deliver a message to you—the granola chick (the woman I was engaged to)—you need to get rid of her. I'm sorry to be blunt, but we are all in agreement. She doesn't understand where you are going and doesn't want to go there."

I was, of course, taken aback but, at the same time, flattered that he thought I was heading to a good place. A long silence ensued as I absorbed this information.

Dick continued, "We also put some thought into who you should marry, and we think it should either be Gordon's daughter, Lauren, or that ski racer, Kristi Terzian." I had generally been skeptical of my father's advice about marriage, which is probably why the group spoke for him. And I was surprised that Dick thought Kristi was even in my range of options. I was certainly aware of Kristi—when I was working in the race department at PCMR in 1992, I watched her race up close, which was amazing. I had watched her special on the Wide World of Sports, which reported on her struggles with injuries and how she continuously crawled back into her position on the World Cup just to have her dreams dashed again just before the Olympics. As part of the mini-documentary, they introduced her mother, who was in a wheelchair with MS. As a skiing enthusiast, I was impressed by her perseverance, fortitude, and courage.

Shortly after we formed POWDR in 1994, I was sitting in my office and had received a bunch of schwag from America's Opening Ski race event. I was pretty excited, so I walked across the hall to consult with my colleague and Marketing officer, Robbie Beck, and Kristi happened to be sitting in Robbie's office at the time. I was excitedly trying on the new schwag and asking for her opinion. Robbie introduced us, and I was so star-struck I acted like a bumbling idiot. Although I didn't hear her say it, I felt like she was thinking, "Who was that goof?" Not a great first impression. But I eventually asked her to a lunch event, and we started a courtship.

When I was ready to introduce her to the family, Dad said, "Are you talking about that frosty ski racer that owns the coffee shop?"

"You do not qualify to advise me about dating and marriage," I replied.

"Boy, you got that right!" Ian confirmed.

Kristi and I were married in 1997 and recently celebrated our twenty-sixth wedding anniversary. She is the strongest woman I know, the love of my life, and I am still star-struck by her. She has been there for me for better or worse, for richer or poorer, in health and in sickness.

The Grand Disappointment.

Elaine Cumming – Granny as a young woman.

David, me and Granny.

My mother, Barbara Darnaby Cumming (Bobbie).

The Three Bears.

Annette and Ian, Jay Nichols and his wife Loretta.

David and I with our nanny, Pierra Bellaviti.

Ian Cumming and Joe Steinberg.

Ian playing the Corporate Raider.

Dad in his bumblebee suit at Snowbird.

Family climbing on Kilimanjaro
(me, Dad, David, cousin Jennifer, Annette)

Ian, me, Annette and David at a wedding.

David, Ian the Wallet Pig, and me.

Boarding school drop off day.

Ian clowning around at the office.

Me, Ian and David floating the Amazon river.

Dad's first time on a snowboard.

Kermit the gulfstream.

Dad doing his happy jig before we started our climb up Mr. Rainier.

Bud Scruggs with Dad.

The Manhole in London.

Ian looking sharp in his bespoke suit.

Dad and I in the tent during the Denali climb.

The strong back, small brain club.
(Robet Link, me, and Win Whittaker)

Dad and I climbing Denali.

Managing the ropes up Denali.

Residual pie crust.

Frozen beneath the tent.

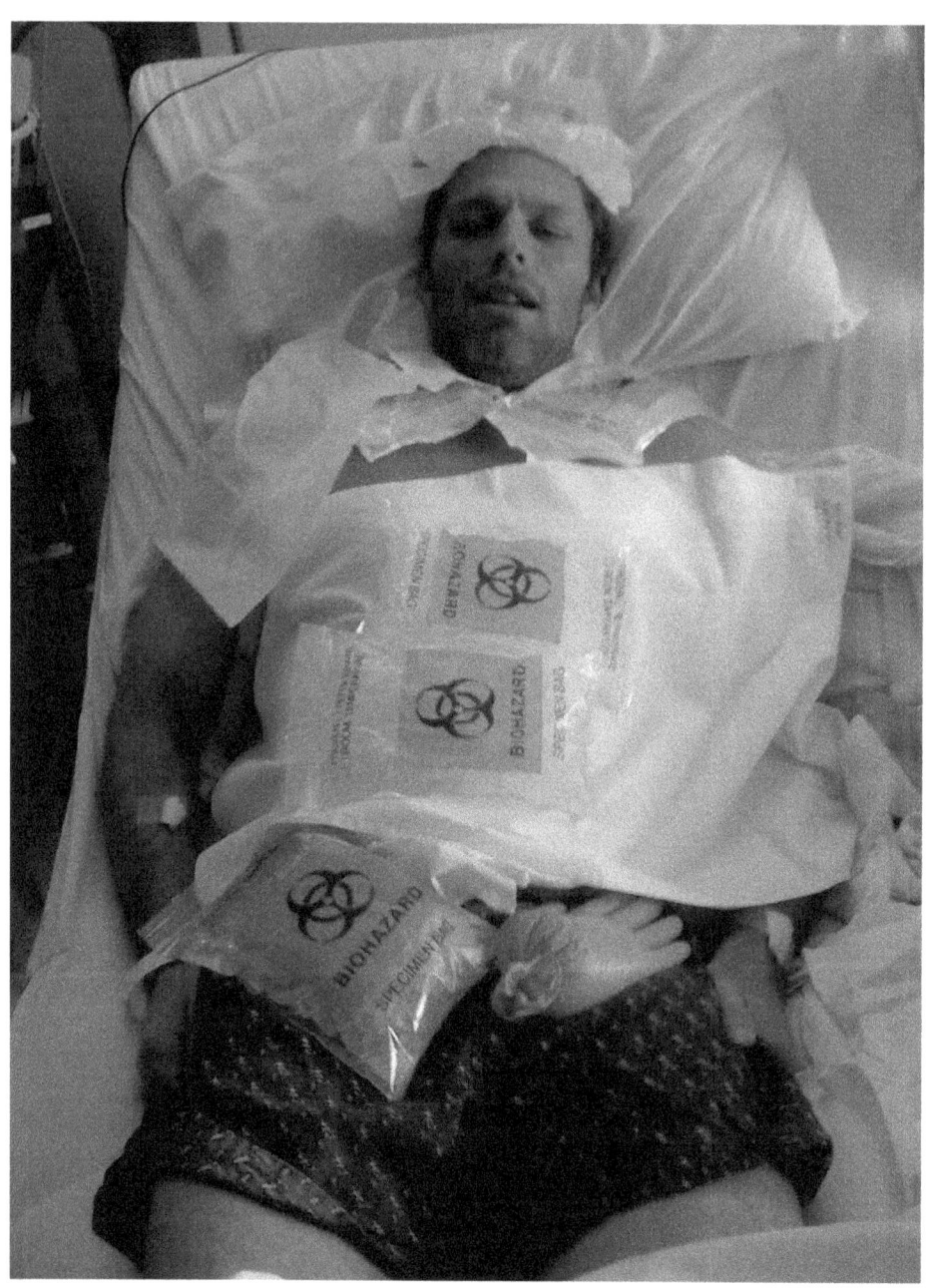

Me, packed in ice.

Dr. Henry McFarland.

Granny bike riding in East Hampton.

Dad in East Hampton, one of his favorite places.

The Shadow of the Mountain

Resilience

"Cut it out, you are as tough as an old boot," Dad said to me for the first time when I was ten years old or so. He repeated the message at a few key points throughout my life when I was experiencing challenges and whining about it. I'm not sure whether he delivered the message as a validation or an aspiration, but his words empowered me to be resilient throughout my life.

Just as I was realizing so many of my life's goals—with a beautiful wife who was pregnant with our son and the career of my dreams—I began having unexplained health issues. One of my selfish passions during my late twenties (which my father disapproved of) was racing cars, and it was during this activity that I noticed the first signs that something wasn't right with my brain and body. I started missing flag stands because I couldn't see them. When I overheated, I would experience a sort of blindness like watching static on the television; the episodes resolved when I was able to cool off. I theorized that I was just out of shape for driving in the heat, so I started wearing more clothes to train, trying to make my body function at higher temperature levels. Things only got worse. Finally, after many months, I went to visit the doctor and said, "I either have a brain tumor or I have MS or something." My family was quite familiar with MS because my mother-in-law had it for years. We did an MRI. The doctor called me a few days later. I was sitting in my office overlooking Main Street in Park City on a beautiful spring ski day in 2000, just a few weeks after my thirty-third birthday. "It looks like you have MS," was his preliminary conclusion. My initial reaction was devoid of emotion. My body felt heavy, and I was in a sort of numb haze. I looked at my assistant who was also on the call and her mouth was still open in a long "O" as if in shock. I ran my hands over my face several times, and in a barely audible, monotone voice I asked her to cancel the rest of my afternoon. Then I slowly drove home. The first image that came to mind and would not leave was me blind and in a wheelchair in the same condition that my mother-in-law was in. I delivered the news to my wife, and I think her response was along the lines of "Shut the fuck up" The irony of both her mother and husband having MS was too cruel. Then I called my father and said simply, "It's MS."

He replied, "Really, are you sure?" I told him I had a meeting with the neurologist next week.

"Fuck that," he said, "We are meeting with the head of neurology at the U (University of Utah) tomorrow." He pulled whatever strings he had through his many connections in Utah, and we met with Dr. John Rose and discussed my diagnosis in more detail. He confirmed that I had two enhancing lesions on my brain and that I did, in fact, have MS. Even though I already knew it, the news had even more of an impact the second time. My face turned ashen, and I heard the voice of a scared child rather than a grown thirty-three-year-old man ask, "Well, what does it mean?"

He responded, "The average MS patient is confined to a wheelchair permanently at about six years after diagnosis. You have a lot of life to live, I recommend you go live it."

I almost flew across the room at him because I felt so violated and furious. Forget the tough old boot. A pure fire propelled me. The doctor was giving me scientific data, but I viewed it as a threat, and my reaction was completely ego/survival driven. I was not going to die; I was going to do everything I could to combat this disease. Hard wind on fire can extinguish a flame; other times it makes the flame go higher. Thank God the wind of my diagnosis ignited fiery rage because, in hindsight, it could have gone the other way. My father had always told me, "Don't curse the darkness, light a fricking match." The gumption that I inherited from my father dictated that I was not going to let this neurologist set my destination on the horizon. I became the junkyard dog like my dad, not willing to accept what I was being told. Ian not only joined the battle, but he also led it. For him, the battle is the victory. It was as if he was made for this moment—his medical school background, his insatiable curiosity, his ability to process vast amounts of information, his connections, and the wealth he had accumulated all came together to help me rise and fight.

As I faced the truth of my new circumstances, I experienced many months of emotional turmoil when my behavior was completely binary—I never knew whether I was going to burst into uncontrollable giggling or fall into rasping sobs in the fetal position on the floor. One of the buoying realities of all the upheaval was my father's approach. Dad sounded the troops and began meeting with everyone he could think of. I'm still not sure how he was able to open the lines of communication that he did, but he threw everything he had at it. He was able to get us meetings with the best thinkers on the subject at the National Institutes of Health (NIH), the greatest research hospital in the country. We started engaging with doctors and researchers, discussing and exploring options together. We learned about autoimmunity at a granular level from scientists in Utah and Washington, D.C. Dad's medical background gave him the ballsy self-assurance to actively debate with every doctor and researcher we met. He was committed to fixing the situation, even though he knew that it might be impossible. He took solace in beating the world into submission. I remember him saying, "Money doesn't matter for much, but when your kid gets sick, it matters."

During this time, I started to have an even greater appreciation for my father's curiosity and his ability to wade through massive amounts of research and synthesize immense volumes of data. It was comforting to externalize the disease as a separate entity that we were strategizing to defeat, as opposed to something that was happening in my own body. His actions gave both of us hope, and I realized that I had a lot of fight left in me. Even if I lost part of that fight, maybe I could assimilate into my father's world by doing something less physical but perhaps equally fulfilling. Sometimes things feel desperate, but if you keep your eye on the horizon, by and large things will work out.

We met with Dr. Henry McFarland, M.D., who was the Chief of the National Institute of Neurological Disorders and Stroke (NINDS), Neuroimmunology Branch, and Dr. Roland Martin, M.D., another brilliant scientist working at NINDS. Many years later, Henry would help with Dad's MCI (mild cognitive impairment) diagnosis, and he became like an uncle to me. During one of our meetings, which had become monthly at that point, Henry mentioned some interesting work being done with stem cell transplants and autoimmunity at Northwestern University by a doctor named Richard Burt. I could see Dad banking the information away. During our next visit, Henry told us that Dr. Burt was putting together a protocol for MS using hematopoietic stem cell transplant (HSCT) but needed to get an endorsement so that he could start a broader trial.

Henry told us, "They claim that they are resetting the immune function in the patients to such a degree that they are not getting inflammation on their brain."

Dad responded, "Does it work?"

Henry explained that they didn't know yet because they needed to obtain pre- and post-transplant blood work to prove the chemistry had changed to get approval.

In his no-nonsense way, Dad said, "So let's get the bloods and figure this out, give me Dr. Burt's number."

Ian worked with Henry, Roland, and Richard to fund the protocol through his foundation and get the information they needed to clear the way for this experimental procedure. He was the catalyst to get the ball rolling and push it through the system. At one point Dad said to me, "There is a lot we don't know, but my instinct is that this is the right thing to do for you"—and he was right.

After six to twelve months, NIH was able to confirm Richard's results. Roland Martin looked at Dad and said, "If my son had MS, I would want him to do this." Amidst huge uncertainty, Dad was able to process the information available, help overcome obstacles, and make a plan. The road had been cleared for me to get a stem cell transplant. I was only the thirteenth patient to do so in the United States. Since then, the Cumming Foundation has paid for many more people to get the procedure.

Shortly after my diagnosis, feeling lost, I thought Susan the Shrink might be a good resource. "I have been diagnosed with MS; my emotions are all over the place. I think I must be depressed." She advised me that I was scared and angry, my go-to emotions since childhood, and the best way to handle it was to accept the death of John Cumming as I believed him to be. My nostrils flared and my eyes bulged—yet another doctor was telling me to sit back and accept my fate! I rejected this immediately with almost the same reaction that I had with Dr. Rose, but I tried to temper my response a bit by covering my mouth with both hands. I reverted to my de facto rules of life, learned during my time as a guide and climber.

I finally snapped back: "We go through life with heavy loads and light loads. My load just got a little heavier, but I'm going to continue to climb like I always do." Susan was trying to get me to stop being me, and all I wanted was to hold onto me. I was not yet in a place of acceptance. Maybe I never would be. I continued to throw myself into the battle with the help of my father. That is what Cummings do—we throw ourselves against challenges that might seem insurmountable in work and life, and we just keep going. In waging war, we are healing ourselves, despite the riskiness of the outcome.

My shrink had been right about one thing—for the procedure to work, they basically did have to kill the old John Cumming. The immune system is like an onion; at the core of the onion are the long-term immune controls. This is where the immune system stores its knowledge of the body's historical exposures. Some immunity can be passed down to us from our mother, or it can be acquired through a vaccine, or by actually surviving a virus as a child. As we age, the various new layers continue to evolve and protect the body as we are exposed to more "environmental insults." With MS, instead of protecting the body, the immune system ironically starts attacking the General of the body, the brain. In the case of stem cell transplantation, the doctors strip the onion down to the first two to three layers and then put new stem cells in with the hope that they will develop a new blood and immune system. The hope is that whatever layer of the onion that decided the brain was the enemy will be destroyed and reset.

Stem cell replacement therapy comes in two types: autologous, which means the stem cells come from the same person who will get the transplant, so the patient is their own donor, and allogeneic, which means the stem cells are from a person other than the patient, either a matched-related or unrelated donor. Both procedures require a near-lethal dose of cyclophosphamide (a chemotherapy drug). The allogeneic method has more associated risks because it requires radiation and is, therefore, a more extensive procedure. It is mostly used for leukemia patients. After three years of research and doctor meetings, I opted for the autologous treatment in 2003.

The first part of the procedure would require harvesting my stem cells. A month later, I would receive an 80% lethal dose of chemo to target and kill the young cells that were propagating and growing in my blood and attacking my brain. This would also restart my immune system. Some blood stem cells are born in bone marrow, mostly in long bones like the femur and lumbar spine, and the goal is to generate high levels of those cells. The doctors gave me a dose of growth hormone and one dose of chemo—the two together work to help the bone marrow start producing more stem cells. After that treatment, I went back to my hotel, where my back, femurs, and pelvis were achy and sore as my body worked overtime to create cells. I returned to the hospital a couple of days later and they performed a bunch of tests to see whether I had produced a sufficient amount of stem cells. The blood work indicated that things were going in the right direction, so they set me up at the harvesting station, which entailed my being in a bed with both arms strapped down flat out, like Jesus on the cross, with needles in my arms and a catheter in the lower region. I tried to focus on my eventual resurrection instead of my current state of pseudo-hospital crucifixion. One needle drew the blood out so it could be spun around to separate the new stem cells, and the needle in the other arm put the rest of the cells back into my body. The whole procedure took about four hours. Being a goal-oriented sort of person, I asked how many cells they had harvested, and they told me around seven million!

"Wow, that's quite a bit!" I said.

"It's about average," the nurse responded blandly. Always keeping me humble.

During the next month at home, while my stem cells were being processed, I felt a little weak and lost some hair, but life was not too bad. I returned to the hospital for the next phase of treatment, which was going to be the hardest. The idea is to reset your immune system by killing the blood, but you can't kill the patient, so it is a fine balance that is constantly being monitored. Returning to the onion analogy, how much chemo the doctors give you determines how many layers of the onion they kill. They want to take you as close to neutropenia as possible, which means having only the immunity that you were born with. Many tests were performed to determine blood chemistry, antibodies, etc. so they could come as close as possible to the lethal dose of cyclophosphamide, without it being too much.

I sat in my hospital room at Northwestern University (NWU), watching the snow blowing off Lake Michigan, thinking of Kristi, who was in the hotel across the street, as the nurse attached the IV filled with poison. They couldn't put that amount of chemo into the distal veins because they would literally melt, so they used a peripherally inserted catheter (PICC) line that went directly to my heart. I closed my eyes as it dripped slowly into my body knowing that for the next ten days, I would be dying. Kristi was five months pregnant with our twin girls at the time, and our son was only three. Because of her condition and mine, she was not allowed to visit me in the hospital. She wanted to be as close to me as possible, so she got a corner room in the hotel right across the street from NWU where my room was, and she would flick the light on and off so I could tell what room she was in. She stood in the window of the hotel talking to me on the phone, and I stood in the hospital window talking to her. All we could see were the silhouettes of each other: Kristi with her large pregnant belly and me a skinny MS patient fighting for his life. Kristi is the strongest woman I've ever known, and she was there to support me in the best and only way she could. We tried to keep our conversation light, but the tone was serious. Thinking of our young family added a whole other level of gravity to the situation. But it also bolstered me, in a way. I needed to be my best self for them and for me, and whatever was coming my way in terms of pain was worth it.

After the first infusion, I got on the stationary bike I had brought into my room for about thirty minutes and went straight back to bed. The team performed more tests and configurations and repeated the IV the next day. On day two I got on the bike for about ten minutes and then collapsed in bed. The bike would continue to sit, unridden, and taunt me for the remainder of my stay in the hospital. After the second day, I started getting very sick, and by day three I was vomiting, having diarrhea, and I could hardly get out of bed. By day four, I was like a naked mole rat, pale and shaky. It takes another four to five days after that to achieve full neutropenia. It was during this phase of the transplant that I was at the most risk; I was weak and severely anemic, and any common infection could have killed me. Consequently, I was in complete isolation, like the boy in the bubble. Hospital staff who came and went had to scrub and put on gloves, gowns, masks, shields, hats, and sterile covers for their feet.

Finally, I was ready for the last phase, returning the propagated stem cells back to my body. The procedure should only take about fifteen minutes. Unfortunately, I had a strange reaction to my cells. All I remember is a room full of people moving around in hazmat suits and feeling like I was going to die. I was mentally calm, but my body went into a complete tailspin with convulsions, fever spikes, vomiting, diarrhea, uncontrollable hiccups, etc. Before my nurse gave me Demerol to effectively knock me out, I remember her looking me in the eyes and saying, "We've got you."

When I woke up a couple of days later, the sterile hospital room was empty and eerily dark, the only sign of life was Dr. Richard Burt, sitting quietly under a single, small spotlight, reading. Richard has gigantic, brilliant blue eyes and he looked up at me calmly and said, "Well, Hello." I thought I had died, and he was God, welcoming me to what I hoped was heaven.

"You gave us a little scare, but now you're back." He said.

The next two weeks in the hospital were rough. I still couldn't see my family and I was fatigued and worn out, but I was no longer afraid. I had been scared for three years, but I had also been crusading shoulder to shoulder with my father creating hope and indefatigable optimism. Ian had used equal parts curiosity, determination, and outright brashness to create catharsis for both of us, and we had gotten the best possible treatment available for me.

Finally, the doctors told me that as long as I masked everywhere I went and watched what I ate (no live culture or raw food), I could be discharged and recover for the next thirty days at home. When Dad came to pick me up at the hospital, I was masked and hooded, dressed like an ER doc during COVID-19. As I entered the waiting area, I saw Dad on his cell phone, in the middle of another deal. I was standing there in my hazmat suit, and he was in his usual business attire talking on the phone giving me the "wait a minute finger." I hadn't seen my family in weeks. I was out of the hospital but still not out of the woods. He wasn't in the room when I thought I was dying, and he didn't seem to acknowledge that I was still frail and at risk. I had just been through one of the most profound experiences of my life, and he had a call to take.

Heat shot through me, and I lost it on him, "We are going right now, hang up your phone!"

When I blew, he knew not to mess with me. We got in the car, and he just returned to his phone call. He was convinced that what we were doing was right, it was done, and now I was healing. My part, your part. "Onward!" Ian was a man of action, and he felt like his part was done. Now it was time for me to do my part and heal. While he had fought for me to get into the trial and had a basic understanding of the science, I don't know if he understood the vulnerability and threat of infection

I faced *after* the procedure. He always had my back but was perhaps not always there emotionally in the way I needed him. This was the light and shadow of Ian's personality that sometimes drove me crazy. I have chosen to be a more emotionally involved father, but I don't begrudge my father his actions on that day at the hospital, it was part of his unapologetic personality.

Neither of us suspected at the time that he would need to step in and save my life again.

Can You Die from the Hiccups?

After taking only that first summer off to recover, I was back at it. Raising young kids, riding my bike like a madman, building POWDR largely through acquisitions in the United States, and living my life. In hindsight, I probably didn't let myself fully recover. About three years after the first stem cell transplant, I started having some symptoms that I had equated with my initial diagnosis. These included light shows in my eyes, severe fatigue, cold, clammy appendages, and strange electric shocks that felt like static was traveling up and down my spine making it difficult to walk. My goal had always been to stay ahead of the disease and react quickly, so when something went wrong or I felt like I might be relapsing, I went directly to the doctor. I was familiar with the mechanisms of the disease and the therapies. I was actively involved with helping other patients get treated, so I had a lot of credibility and (outsized) influence at the University of Utah. I went to my neurologist for another MRI. This time it was with a different scanner and a different protocol from last time—it was with the preconceived notion that *this was an MS patient who was probably having a recurrence of MS*, instead of, *this patient is having some issues, let's see what's going on*. In hindsight, the scan was probably inconclusive, and I should have gotten a second opinion.

Pre-transplant, I was using a monoclonal antibody drug that had a reasonably good effect for a while; I assumed that I was having a recurrence and suggested that I go back on this drug. The doctor agreed to put me back on the antibody drug, but he administered it at the same level that I had been on before the transplant, which my brand-new immune system was not accustomed to. I went in for about two to three infusions but was also trying to work and keep up with my life. I was in Killington, one of the resorts we had recently acquired in Vermont, at a meeting with our executive team and board of directors talking about our plans for the future. Throughout the two-hour session, I felt this weird popping in my right ear and developed a severe sore throat, also on the right side. I reached up and ran my hand over a lump the size of a golf ball on my neck. Next, I had a shooting pain in the right side of my groin, where another lymph node had blown up to the size of an egg.

Finally, I leaned over and whispered to my colleague, Paul Rowsey, "I'm kind of sore and feeling a little sick and can you see this lump on my neck?"

Paul took one look and said, "Get on a plane and get your ass home to the doctor."

On my way back across the country, the nodes under both arms blew up, I spiked a high fever and felt like I was in a scene from the science fiction horror film, *Scanners*. Over the next year, I would be in and out of the hospital many times with a whole array of symptoms. I discovered that when lymph nodes rupture, which happened several times, it causes a spike in uric acid, which leads to severe gout. My fingers, toes, neck, back, and most of my joints were swollen due to the crystalized uric acid in my body. I would repeatedly spike 104-degree fevers, and they would have to pack me in ice to cool me down. As the fevers came on, I would start shivering, which led to convulsions called rigor. On several occasions these events caused me to lose consciousness. The doctors administered opioids for the pain and steroids for the inflammation. But there were times when I would also appear completely fine; the vicissitudes of the situation were utterly maddening, for me and the doctors. Oftentimes, before the convulsions would start, I would get weird, wracking hiccups that would leave me breathless for about forty-five seconds.

One day, Dad was visiting me at our home in Park City. We were walking around the house because I always felt like movement aided my body; it also seemed to help break fevers and gave me a goal. As we were walking and talking, I collapsed on the ground, gasping for air. After a few minutes, I started walking again, only to have the same thing happen. That time it knocked the wind out of me; it felt like a three-hundred-pound tackle had just plowed over me. Dad was following me around, worried as hell, and trying to comfort me. I tried to get up for a third time, and my body buckled. I was on all fours panting like a dog with my tongue out as Dad was trying to help me onto the couch. He had my General Practitioner on speed dial, and as I was about to lose consciousness, I heard my dad talking to Dr. Tom Miller,

"I'm sorry to bother you, Tom, but John's having another episode, and I don't know what I should do?" His voice grew smaller, like that of a young boy as he inquired, "Has anyone ever died of the hiccups?"

For some reason, through the pain and anxiety, I found this hysterical. Self-assurance was something Dad was never short of, but on that day, it was like kryptonite had entered the room. We were both broken down into our core elements. When I was admitted to the hospital again in the spring of 2008 at the University of Utah, I was packed in ice to reduce my fever. I was surrounded by infectious disease doctors who were asking me all kinds of bizarre inquiries that seemed completely irrelevant to what was happening at the time. There was also a staff of neurologists and a variety of other specialists. I was dying, and they couldn't figure out what was going on. My dad entered the mix and became more anxious when he saw my deteriorating condition; he gave my hand a quick squeeze, so I knew he was there with me. He immediately dialed Dr. Henry McFarland.

"Are you aware of what's going on here?" Ian proceeded to describe the scene around him. Henry quickly determined that the initial scan was probably bad and instructed my dad and my neurologist to immediately "get the infectious disease guys out of the room" and start a maximum dose of catabolic steroids. The monoclonal antibody that I had been taking was cloned from a mouse molecule and had been manipulated to be undetectable by the human immune system. But my *new* immune system was screaming, "Hey wait, why are you injecting all of that mouse into me, I am going to kill it!" My body went berserk. It was a combination of too high a dose and my new immune system overreacting. It was like a massive lupus attack where the immune system attacked every tissue in my body; it was full-on anarchy. Ian later told me that he overheard one of the doctors say, "If we give him that much Solumedrol, it will kill him," Henry's response was, "If we don't, he's dead." Within an hour of my first bag of max dose Solumedrol (catabolic steroid), I was talking like I had just woken up from the weirdest dream. Henry and my father saved my life, again.

What I needed was another stem cell transplant, but the doctors didn't want to use chemo again, so they chose a protocol of a maximum dose of Solumedrol to reset my immune system. Technically it was not a stem cell transplant, but it was effectively the same thing. Steroids suppressed my immune system to the same level that chemo had done. Different drug, same result. When I received the maximum dose of the intravenous steroid, I was told it would take approximately eighteen months to taper off because the kidneys couldn't handle it. But it wasn't a precise taper, and when we tapered too fast, the withdrawal was far worse than anything I had experienced in my life. As we stopped the IV and shifted to the oral dose, I went through severe withdrawal—crying, shaking, and uncontrollably emotional, which somehow brought out the young child in me. I went back to the hospital, completely out of it and irrational. They finally knocked me out with Demerol until I could get through the worst of the withdrawal symptoms, but I was still in the hospital for a while. During that time, I would look forward to the visits from my dad; he gave me self-assurance, reassurance, and hope. Kristi was supportive and visited as much as she could, but she was also busy raising three young children without much help from me because of the illness. When Dad didn't show up for a couple of days, I called his office and discovered he was in London! WTF! I was so livid that I stewed in resentment for another few days before calling him. When he answered, he sounded slightly fearful—he knew that I would be running hot-tempered. "You are so fiery!" he would often tell me. Upon hearing his voice, I realized that I was being silly. London was his meditation; staying in a fancy hotel, eating kippers, walking around Saville Row—this is what soothed him when he was worried.

"Hey Dad, are you having kippers?" I asked.

"Yup."

"Are you staying at The Connaught?"

"Yup."

"Maybe you can pick up a suit for me?"

"I think you have one more fitting," he said.

"I'll be there as soon as I can."

We both knew it was a joke about a sports coat he had gotten me in high school, but it was familiar and we both chuckled.

Finally, they got the dosage right and I went home. In hindsight, maybe I knew too much. I was still active in the MS world, helping other patients, and trying to influence the neurology department at the U. If I hadn't been so involved, maybe my neurologist would not have accommodated me when I wanted to go back on monoclonals. After the second transplant (which is not what it really was but what it seemed like), I felt like I had been through hell and back. As I eased back into normal life, I would see friends who would say, "Huh—looks like you lost some weight." Life goes on, it doesn't matter.

As Dad would say, "Pass the potatoes!"—everyone is wrapped up in their world, so don't take yourself so seriously. It is easy to lament what is broken; during the arc of life, you acquire wisdom and perspective, and enduring the hard moments makes you realize that nothing is permanent. If you have the strength to wait, hope will rise again. Dad bolstered me genetically—with a high tolerance for pain, a strong will to survive and carry on, and a short memory for hellish experiences—and mentally, through his words and actions. He helped me realize that I had a lot to offer despite my diagnosis, such as the intellectual plasticity and energy to learn everything that I could and the audacity and egocentricity to think that somehow my story mattered and maybe I could make a difference in the world if only I could stay alive.

The Consolation Prizes

My internal fire got me through my initial MS diagnosis and many days after that when I was desperately scared. But a few key people in my life further helped me digest my diagnosis and translate that rage into action. My father's old friend, Bud Scruggs, called me repeatedly after my diagnosis; I avoided his calls for a while because I was just trying to get through the days. I didn't want help yet, and I didn't want to talk to him or anyone else at that point. He was persistent and finally, in exasperation, I answered his call and we agreed to meet for lunch. He divulged some of his life challenges, and that he had found that the Mormon Church provided comfort when he needed it through common values and community. He was deeply challenged as a young man and many times he screamed to the universe, "WHY ME??" He explored it for many years and came up with the only answer, which is "WHY NOT ME?" Bud emphasized the importance of this type of mindset; emotional dire straits can go south quickly, and you can't wallow there. His message to me had nothing to do with religion, it was a practical way to look at life. Sometimes people don't want to get near the problems of others, but Bud reached out and kept reaching out until he got to me. I needed another arm to grab onto outside of my family, and he offered his arm as a friend. This gesture meant the world to me. He remains to this day a mentor and loving friend, and I talk to him all the time about life, philosophy, business, etc. Bud told me, "The minute you start looking too closely at your own story, you defeat the benefit and perspective that you should receive." This led me to the enlightened conclusion that everyone has "stuff," and the universe didn't care about mine. I started feeling less sorry for myself, but I still needed to find something to help me gain equanimity with the disease that was living in my body.

My dad suggested I talk to his friend, Michael Zimmerman, who is a reputable lawyer, a Chief Justice on the Utah Supreme Court, and someone I had climbed with in the past. What I didn't know about Mike was that he was also a Buddhist monk. We talked extensively, and with him as my guide, I studied Buddhism more thoroughly. We even met with the Dalai Lama at one point who, remarkably, gave me the same insight as Bud.

With the utmost respect to this spiritual monolith, I uttered, "I have MS and I'm desperately scared."

He shrugged and smiled and said it was a matter of perspective. "Members of my faith would be thankful to know what their karma suggests."

Why not you? Who do you think you are? Embrace your reality as if you chose it.

My search continued—not for an answer to "Why Me" but for acceptance within myself.

Mitt Romney was transitioning into his role with the 2002 Olympics and had heard about my situation with MS from Dick Marriott. I was stunned when he called me a couple of months into my research. He informed me that his wife, Anne, also had MS. She had wholeheartedly adopted Eastern medicine (energy work) and alternative approaches to dealing with her disease. She had found a doctor in Park City, Utah, that she swore by, an acupuncturist named Dr. Ding.

"She goes at least once a month, and since you live in Park City, I thought you should know that he is there," Mitt said.

I've been seeing Dr. Ding since that day.

A "glimpse" is a Zen Buddhist event that comes to you periodically if you follow a dedicated meditation practice. Meditation provides the space for these flashes to occur. With the help of the three humans mentioned above, I was able to occasionally be in that space. One day when I was meditating, I had a glimpse of something I call the consolation prize. Did I want the grand prize of a long healthy life? Of course I did, but there are other prizes. Throughout fighting this progressive disease, I essentially lost three lines on the eye chart overnight, was agonized by weeks of bed spins, watched chemo chemicals being dripped into my veins, and washed all the hair off my body one morning. I went through countless MRIs, experimental drugs, and two stem cell transplants where I was in a sterile bubble for weeks. But what I would gain during this process was a much greater depth of perspective into what it means to be a human being. I had empathy and compassion because I had faced astounding levels of fear. I could see myself in the context of the world, and quite frankly, the fact that the universe didn't care about me or who I thought I was, was humbling. Suffering adds depth of character, uncertainty provides appreciation. These were qualities that would ultimately make me a better man. At that time, would I have traded the prizes for a different diagnosis? Probably, but now I wouldn't trade them for the world.

We all experience a gamut of emotions in our lifetime because our brains are designed to send these messages through thoughts. We have painful experiences, challenges, setbacks, and fear, and during those times the equal and opposite energy is also ignited/illuminated within us. Equanimity, sanguinity, empathy, and compassion are things I would never have received had I not suffered so profoundly from the fear of losing myself. The person I thought I was continues to disappear, and I have to reckon with that. The consolation prize for enduring the degradation of function, the acceleration of aging, and the frustration I experience daily is an intense understanding of myself and the people around me.

I know all of this, and I value the consolation prizes, but I am a human being, and I still suffer from self-doubt, negativity, and judgment (of myself and those around me). Some days I can still be the selfish young man that I was in my twenties, the one that my father cut off; other days I yell at my kids or I'm short with my wife. I judge myself very harshly for not having the constant benefit of the exalted outlook on life that I have been granted; it makes me angry and discouraged. The panorama of my existence is richer, broader, and has more texture and wisdom than it otherwise would have, but I am not an exemplar. "Why Me" would indicate that I was chosen somehow, and "Why Not Me" reflects the truth of my humanity, that I am flawed, like my father and like everyone else. The consolation prizes I received are not limitless, unchallenged powers; I am in a perpetual balancing act between being cognizant of the gifts and forgiving myself when I don't always use them. I have learned to grade myself more or less on a curve. My father taught me this early on in life when I was to be known as the "son of a wealthy father." But MS introduced me to a whole new bell curve. After more than twenty years with this disease, I have to let go of the competitive aspirations that were once so important to me. I'm legally blind in one eye, my balance is off, and my stamina is waning. I have to embrace the battle and persevere. Some days when I ski with a group, I'm a little slower and I might not make it down, but hell, it is a victory that I am even out there on the slopes. The rest of the world might not be so forgiving, so I need to be more empathetic, and remember the words of my father, "Quit being so hard on yourself."

Helping Other Patients

While I don't put myself out there publicly for other MS patients, if someone finds their way to me, I take their call 100% of the time. I know what it feels like to be at the bottom of a dark canyon, and it is nearly impossible to get out of the abyss all by yourself. I always try to counsel them because when I went through it, there was very little hope. Few therapies were available, and a broad array of outcomes were possible. Being told that you will end up in a wheelchair in a few short years can put even the most optimistic person in a tailspin. I remember feeling as though I were drowning, and the doctors, and even other MS patients that I spoke with, were not giving me the emotional raft that I needed. I had to learn to utilize self-reliance and other skills to quickly navigate the uncertainty of my future.

Consequently, my approach to talking to other patients begins with a wholehearted, emotional hug. My father almost always started our interactions with a warm, open embrace; knowing how reassuring that made me feel, it is the way I start my conversations with other MS patients. First, let's cry together and then we will talk about what you need, which is most often perspective, guidance, friendship, mentorship, and the brass ring (which represents ever-lasting hope). They share their journey and I share mine. The diagnosis happens to the whole family, and everyone has a different reaction to the disease for a variety of circumstantial reasons.

Some people surrender completely to the burden and let it overcome them; their identity becomes MS. They gain power in the world by having this story and it provides leverage for them. While I am sympathetic to this approach, it is not the perspective I chose to frame my chronic illness. Not a moment goes by that I am not dealing with this disease, but I try hard every day not to be an MS patient. It is an aspect of who I am, a part of my story, but it does not define me. From the very beginning, I resented being objectified as a statistic, and that feeling drives me to this day. In other conversations, I find a kindred spirit, someone who accepts the torch and wants to run with it, someone with the resilience and fight to find another way. I do my best to offer information and reinforcement, so they can be invigorated to forge their path ahead. The foundation that my father set up has helped fund the same treatment that I received years ago for many patients each year, and we are proud of what we have been able to accomplish.

Copper Moose Farm

After my stem cell transplants, I had an immune system equivalent to that of a two-week-old infant and the recovery was brutal. I knew that I had to treat my body holistically and with the greatest of care. Many autoimmune issues stem from inflammation related to the digestive system, and so I deduced that if I could control what went into my body, it would (hopefully) have a positive impact on my overall health and speed up my recovery from the procedures. Further research enlightened me about the presence of net consumers and net contributors. Net consumers are typically refined, or processed foods filled with chemicals that are difficult for the body to assimilate. On the opposite spectrum, net contributors represent things like organically grown vegetables, which are pure, efficient, evolutionarily appropriate, and easier for the body to process. The net-net was that I needed to fill my body with net contributors.

The demands of a growing world population have made it necessary to process food and ship it all over the world. The result is that food is plentiful but has become less nutritious (particularly our produce) and generates a huge carbon footprint. To deliver fruits and vegetables across the globe, a tomato (for example) is grown in a warm climate on a mechanized farm with depleted soil quality; it is subjected to pesticides and is likely derived from GMOs. It is then harvested a month before it is ready—which reduces its nutritional value considerably. The tomato travels through a processor to be waxed, dyed, and prepared for transport by trucks, boats, and planes to places where a tomato hasn't grown in six months because it is out of season. The reddish-orange sphere on the produce shelf that resembles a tomato possesses none of the nutritional value of a tomato and also permanently marked the earth with a carbon footprint the size of a Mack truck. The main takeaway from our analysis was that our food is no longer nutritional, and to deliver it harms our environment.

For months, I ranted and raved about how broken and harmful the food production and delivery system in this world had become. I drove my friends and family crazy with lectures about the problem. At some point, I recalled the words of my father, saying "John, quit ranting and do something about it. Don't curse the darkness, light a match!" Once that revelation came to me, the work began. This would be my version of planting the trees to neutralize my existence, but it was going to be a little more public and it would selfishly serve the health of me and my family.

Kristi and I plunged into learning about how food arrives on the grocery store shelves and what we could do differently to restore nutrition while minimizing the environmental impact. The answer was to somehow provide super nutritional foods that were sourced and grown locally with minimum impact on the environment and distributed to a much smaller radius—like our community in Park City. So, in 2006, Kristi and I started a local community organic farm. Farming in the high desert of Utah? It can be challenging and is most definitely a labor of love, but our vision came to fruition through a lot of trial and error, hard work, education, and, of course, a great team to make it happen!

We decided to create our farm using local soil and local microbes with the goal of delivering food to our community within hours of harvesting it. At the time, there were a few co-op gardens and community-supported agriculture (CSA) organizations popping up, but the mainstream farm-to-table movement had not gained significant momentum, at least not in Utah. We were lucky enough to be able to conduct this experiment using our land, so that was the first part of a difficult equation. We threw ourselves into finding the most environmentally friendly methods for growing produce at an elevation of 7,000 feet, including hydroponics, greenhouse technologies, and a building technique for the greenhouse called Earthship biotecture. This unique technology creates structures that are zero-consumption: they consume no net water or power, produce no net carbon dioxide, and use almost no energy. The front of the greenhouse is made of glass that allows sunlight to come through, and the remaining walls are made of tires backed by a berm of dirt. It is designed to insulate the building from the natural variability in outside temperatures. Rooftop systems collect rainwater and filter it into cisterns to water the plants.

We hired a wonderful woman named Daisy (the garden goddess) who possessed vast experience with this sort of gardening and an environmental science degree from the University of Utah. We started as a small CSA with no more than twenty families as we honed our technique and proceeded down the learning curve of what worked and what didn't. Currently, we have more than one hundred members and a waiting list. We have fourteen employees and volunteers, and we provide produce to some local restaurants. We also built a farm stand where other community members can buy vegetables, flowers, and other local artisanal foods during the summer months. Our measures for success included three things: (1) to produce tasty, edible, nutritional food; (2) to give life to a sustainable community asset; and

(3) to achieve the operational breakeven point in our cash flow at some point. The best-case scenario for the environment would be that everyone copied us, and we got driven out of business because there was so much competition! More community farms have popped up in Park City these days, but we are still in business and adding new products to our mix every year.

We are proud that we established an organic farm that serves our community in a way that is ecologically, nutritionally, and environmentally friendly. Local families pick their own wholesome produce in the greenhouse, and even a few tourists visit the farm stand to sample locally grown vegetables, homemade desserts, fresh eggs, and artisanal cheeses. We're doing the best we can to make ourselves and our environment enduring and sustainable in every aspect, and of all the things I have been involved with in my life, Copper Moose Farm is one of the most satisfying. And we think it makes the meadowlarks happy too!

To Climb Another Day

The Rubber Tire Market

Having MS does not define me, but I cannot deny the impact it has had on my life. While I was dealing with diagnosis and treatment, I was also raising a young family with my wife and trying to expand my business. It was an incredibly busy, stressful time, but the work ethic and drive I inherited from my father propelled me forward. My quest to bring the mountain lifestyle to others only became more pertinent and I forged ahead with my goals for POWDR.

The ski industry offers limited areas of growth, and one of the primary ways is through acquisition. The premiere destination resorts would always trade amongst themselves, and POWDR didn't have the capital to play in that game early on. But Nick Badami had laid the groundwork for the way I thought about smaller resorts, which he called, "community gems." Such resorts were usually family-owned and part of the "rubber tire market." The latter term implied that it was a mountain that families drove to, usually with their lunch in a cooler. Nick speculated that if we operated efficiently, provided good value to the constituents, and were good stewards of the community gems, we could establish a foothold and improve the resorts with investments over time. Just as my father and his company rooted out undervalued businesses that needed to be fixed or sold off, we rooted out family ski resorts that had a lot of charm and potential that we could judiciously invest in and make them the best versions of themselves. Similar aspirations, very different processes.

For a while, we were kind of a small player in this niche market, but over time our growth led to us becoming one of the largest private ski holding companies in the world. Moreover, when the pandemic hit, while we suffered in the beginning (as everyone did), we were ultimately in a fortunate position. People were not able to get on a plane and travel, but they could "rubber tire it" to their local ski resort with a brown bag of sandwiches and enjoy an amazing day in the mountains. That is the vibe that made skiing great in the first place, and I'm proud that our community gems ended up being the place where people found refuge from the storm. Being able to enjoy the outdoors is what saved a lot of people during that difficult time, and it is what has always saved me. The following short stories provide highlights about some of POWDR's more notable acquisitions; as the company grew, the successes and challenges we faced allowed me to mature with it.

I Remember You

Everyone has career-changing stories, and the Mount Bachelor acquisition holds great significance for me. From a professional standpoint, the negotiation represents a tremendous learning experience and one of the most intense years of my life. Leading the team that closed this deal demanded intuition, tenacity, strategy, and, of course, balance. For me, it was the ultimate fulcrum.

When we decided to expand our presence in the ski industry, Nick recommended that my research include skiing as many mountains as I could, and that Mount Bachelor should be high on my list. At his suggestion, I traveled to Oregon and was rewarded with a perfect

Bachelor day: the sky was a flawless periwinkle blue after fresh snow had fallen the night before, the pitch of the mountain was superb, the views were sweeping, the terrain unparalleled, and I can still smell the crisp scent of the pine trees. The whole experience invigorated all five of my senses and left an indelible feeling in my mind that I associate with heaven. At the end of that glorious day, I stormed into the management office still covered in snow, and asked to speak with Dave March, who was the general manager at the time. I introduced myself and POWDR and launched into a monologue about our passion for the industry, our aspirations to build something like Bachelor one day, and by the way if he ever wanted to sell the resort to give me a call. Dave smiled and sent me on my way like I was a young buck with a lot to learn (which I was), assuring me that the resort was not for sale.

Five years later, I happened to be sitting at my desk when the phone rang. I don't always answer my phone personally but for some reason this time I did.

"This is Dave March, you probably don't remember me, we met at Bachelor."

To this day, those words give me goosebumps. I said, "Oh, I remember you." I was peripherally aware that something was going on regarding the shareholders at Bachelor, so I suspected the reason for Dave's call was important. Dave was considered one of the major players in the industry and had been tasked with finding a new owner for Bachelor, so the fact that he remembered me and thought of POWDR as a possible suitor made me feel honored. I told him I would be there the next day. I consider that phone call and my serendipitous answering of the call to be a pivotal point in my career.

Mountains are community assets, and everyone feels like they own them, and in this case, many of them actually did. We ended up running a campaign of sorts to influence the shareholders to tender their shares to POWDR. We met with community members and explained our story and philosophy—I often refer to it as the time I ran for mayor! Meanwhile, the other side was actively lobbying and pressuring people to vote in their direction, which created a division in the town.

Ultimately, after eighteen months, we did get the majority of the shares and were able to complete the acquisition. During this time, I was 100% fixated on that project. I sacrificed time with family, and I was grouchy as hell, standing on my tippy toes reaching and doing everything within my power to get that particular brass ring (just as my father had demonstrated), to the exclusion of everything else in my life. And then I got it, and we immediately started looking at the next opportunity. There are days when I wish I didn't have this disease of entrepreneurialism because it is certainly an addiction and uses up a lot of energy, but ultimately it is a blessing that I share with my father. The Bachelor acquisition taught me firsthand many of the things I had learned from my father: to be patient, follow my instincts, deal strategically with a multitude of personalities, and that sometimes getting what you love requires sacrifice.

The Pres and Les Show

Preston Smith and Les Otten were two legends in the industry when I was getting involved. They dominated New England skiing, and as a young man coming up in the industry, I was both intimidated and impressed at their sophistication and audacity. I didn't have the same kind of swagger that they did; I was more of a "better lucky than smart" kind of dude. Pres originally owned Killington and ended up selling it to Les in 1996 when Les formed the American Skiing Company (ASC). At one time I remember Les saying to me, "You should sell me your ski resorts, we are going to put you out of business anyway." Meanwhile, Ian and Nick were of a different mindset, "You can't put $100M into a New England ski resort and expect it's going to take off. You have to make the money to justify the investment. They will all go broke."

Dad's words turned out to be prophetic. Eventually Les became overextended, and ASC ended up being owned by financial institutions, and they were looking to sell. I was ambitious, impulsive, and somewhat insecure as a leader at POWDR. However, I was determined to buy some of what ASC was selling. I was rising before dawn every day, full of adrenaline, talking to anyone who would listen about how we could get a piece of the action. Everyone bought a piece of ASC, sometimes paying as high as ten times cash flow (which was high back then). We were just a small player in the industry at the time, and we were inevitably left out in the snowbank. SOL.

But then I got a phone call from Dave McKown, the New England banker who had worked with Ian at Leucadia and had also helped us finance Mountain Hardware. He had a friend named Paul Rowsey, who through clever means had figured out a way to get control of the real estate in Killington, including the parking lots. I talked with Paul, and he said, "I don't know anything about skiing, but I think this real estate could be worth a lot someday." POWDR went forward in a joint venture with Paul's company and purchased Killington in 2007. Compared to the West, where we had more knowledge and experience, New England skiing was a whole different beast.

We had our key performance indicators (KPI) from the other resorts, and we tried to apply them to the Killington business model. I recruited an old friend and long-time industry operator to help turn things around, named Chris Nyberg. Chris recognized that it was going to take hard, unrelenting work to fix Killington. We were both going to be hated, but we underestimated how bad it would get. My tactics were unpolished, and I had tunnel vision. Our philosophy was to find the studs in the house and start rebuilding. We examined our revenue model, streamlined products, reduced discounts, and compressed the shoulder season operating days. We ruthlessly excised what needed to be reduced, and we did all this with zero communication internally or externally. It was Ian and Nick's motto, "We don't tell them what we are going to do, we tell them what we did." This probably works in some instances, but in the consumer services space, it is a bad idea.

It was management by airstrike. I would fly in, meet with Chris, and things would explode. I would leave, and Nyberg would be left cleaning up the mess. At one point, there were pictures of Chris around town that said, "WANTED DEAD OR ALIVE." We were both wildly unpopular, but he took the brunt of it because he lived there. Meanwhile, Ian was cheering me on from the sidelines because he knew it all had to be done, that it was going to require discipline, and it would be a great education for me. Being a serious person (in Ian's eyes) meant being able to wield the sword when necessary, and that is what needed to be done at Killington. I was ambitious and still somewhat inexperienced. My intense focus on KPIs caused unnecessary damage to the brand, the company, the team, and the community. We basically pooped in our own nest.

My love for the mountains, and my fond experiences of being at Snowbird with my father, was the driver of my work at PCMR, the formation and growth of POWDR, and the realization that the mountains help families like mine be together and enjoy meaningful experiences. And yet, amid this acquisition, I was losing my ability to enjoy all of the things I loved about the mountains due to my health. While I was trying to build an efficient business that would appreciate and improve these mountain experiences, my body was failing me. I was trying to deliver the mountain experience to others, and yet I was losing those experiences for myself. At the same time, I was trying to prove that I had something more to offer society than my physical skills. I wanted to be a good leader and entrepreneur like my father. I wanted to be a good executive like Nick Badami. My wife was one of the world's best skiers, and I wanted to show her that I could build a world-class ski resort. It was against this backdrop that I made some poor decisions and acted in a way that caused me regret.

In hindsight, what we did was the right thing for the business. What I lament is making those decisions so abruptly, without communicating effectively. Had I been more sensitive and patient, the process would have been easier and smoother. Two things seemingly in conflict can be true at the same time—could I have done better? Yes. Was what we did to fix the business wrong? No. I don't regret the necessary tough decisions I made; I regret not doing it with mastery.

"What in the Hell Is a Woodford?"

My father was adept at making difficult decisions by stepping back and taking a macro look at the world around him. Every business experienced difficulty in 2008, and ours was no different. The macro context of our industry was taking several hits at once. In addition to the pressures of a tanking global economy, the ski industry was facing its own challenges: what to do in the face of a changing demographic and reduced utilization rates, how to counteract the effects of climate change, and (on the action sports side) how to safely train athletes to perform in sports where the bar is constantly being raised. While I was acutely aware of these problems, I wasn't sure how to fix them.

Later that year when I was vacationing with my family on the East Coast, I received a call from a colleague who had heard I was looking at complementary businesses and asked if I was interested in meeting with Gary Ream, the founder of Woodward, to visit their flagship camp in Pennsylvania. I still don't know exactly why I agreed to the meeting, but I found myself driving through small farming towns with Amish buggies and horse-drawn hay wagons in western Pennsylvania the following Tuesday morning. I entered the camp and was immediately impressed with the enormous facility. More than eight hundred teenage kids were at summer camp that week, and each one had a marvelous look of rapt attention and focus on their face.

As Gary explained to me, it is a camp designed by the kids for the kids. It had everything a teenager could ever dream of, including a variety of parks for every action sport you can imagine, gymnastics and cheer training facilities, a recording studio, and even a digital media center for creating videos.

My first visit was on a Tuesday, and the experience was so impactful that I went back three more Tuesdays in a row. During those visits, I absorbed the daily rhythms and patterns of the camp and talked to the kids to understand the impact the camp had on their confidence, independence, and fervor for self-expression.

I was hooked, but the key would be convincing the POWDR board, which included my father, of the distinct advantages that Woodward brought to the table and the complementary fit with our existing businesses. I explained that the ski population was aging, and we needed a way to attract Millennial and Generation Z cohorts not only to the ski industry but to the entire resort throughout the year. Climate change and market share wars over pricing could end up debilitating our industry; we needed a solution to counteract these obstacles. As the level of skill and technique required to navigate the terrain park and the half-pipe grew increasingly sophisticated, I felt obliged to safely train athletes to accomplish these feats.

As I relayed my thoughts about the Woodward experience to the board, I could see them trying to understand the fit. My brother David got it right away, but I could see that the rest of the board was struggling. Then my father spoke for the group, "You are in the ski resort business, what in the hell is a Woodford?"

I'm not sure if he didn't hear me correctly or was being humorous, but it was clear that he would have to see the place in person to be convinced. He agreed to take a trip to Pennsylvania to see it for himself and within two minutes of arriving at Woodward, Pennsylvania, he said "Enough, I get it. You are going to change your industry." He took this new information, processed it in his gestalt brain, and when he gave his full support, the rest of the board gave their approval to move forward.

While I felt that I had thoroughly envisioned the progression from outdoor/summer training to mountain activities in the winter, we needed to test that theory in reality, which was when we began construction on the Woodward facility at Boreal. One of our best managers expertly navigated the project and worked with members of the Woodward family to develop a progression that could start with gymnastics and skate parks and go all the way up the mountain where campers would be able to do advanced tricks safely when they left. Since most of the Woodward architects were former campers, we were following the tried-and-true strategy of designing a camp by the kids for the kids! It worked like a dream.

As we look to the future, we see the integration of Woodward into our daily resort business as fundamental to our success as a company. Adding Woodward to our blend of resorts not only creates a unique value proposition that differentiates us from our competitors but also fosters more practitioners who are committed to us over a longer time. Perhaps most importantly, Woodward allows POWDR to offer the next generation a place to have safe adventures and express themselves creatively. We were definitely on a high from the series of acquisitions that had strengthened our company and our knowledge base. But our load was about to get a lot heavier.

The Lease

I have never in my adult life cried as hard as when I had to ask my father and my brother to meet me at the family office late in the fall of 2011. The office was vacant, unnervingly still, and dark. I wanted to look them in the eyes when I told them that I had blown our business up—that the complicated network of leases in place that allowed us to run our ski business at PCMR had been somehow—unbelievably—mishandled and we were in a highly vulnerable position that we would probably not win.

The upper part of what was known as the Park City Ski Area was owned by United Park City Mines (UPCM), a successful silver mining corporation that had consolidated a bunch of smaller mines into one entity. When Nick Badami came to town in the 1970s, the mining industry had long since started to wane, but skiing on Treasure Mountain was gaining momentum as a tourist attraction in Park City. Additionally, Nick's son, Craig, had shown an interest in running ski resorts, and Nick was eager to start a family business during his retirement. UPCM owned the asset but running a ski operation was not in their wheelhouse, so they weren't quite sure how to make the highest and best use of the asset. Nick did not have a lot of capital, but he had a sharp, quantitative mind, and he saw an opportunity for his family to extend their ski resort assets (they already owned Alpine Meadows in Tahoe). He came up with an innovative strategy to get control of the land through a multi-level lease structure that allowed the Badami family to create a top-notch ski resort and UPCM to earn a favorable ROI on their asset. It is not uncommon to rent ski land, but usually, a state or federal government owns the land, and the leases are long—with an autorenewal clause. This arrangement was different—creative, and it served its purpose—but it was complicated and required someone to monitor the renewal. Nick officially acquired the property in 1975 and worked over the next fifteen years to make the resort and the community a highly sought-after ski destination.

When the Cumming family came into the picture and we established the POWDR corporation with Nick in 1994, one of the things we discussed at length was the fact that these leases were key to the business and should not be overlooked. Nick eventually stepped down, and I became CEO and was in charge of running the resort. I had my head down trying to grow the business. Much like my father, I clutched the notes I had from the classes I had taken during my own HBS experience and was determined to put them to work. In our corporate value-setting exercises the number one value was ENDURING. At the time, for me, that translated into a maniacal need to reduce unnecessary costs so we could put the money back into the mountain—improved grooming, restaurants, reliable staff, and lifts. We were committed to providing a gold-standard level of service and having a positive relationship with our community; our focus was on preserving the resort and the mountain for posterity. We invested thoughtfully in the resort, and we certainly benefited from the tide that swept through Park City during the 1990s and early 2000s when we hosted Olympic events. What was once a sleepy mining town had become a top-ten resort. We also invested heavily in the community in a variety of ways, but mostly by creating the Park City Community Foundation. My family lived in Park City full-time, and we wanted to make sure the resort and the town thrived in every way.

During this time, UPCM realized that the value of their land had increased dramatically. They came to us offering to sell the land, but to stick to my mission I wanted to focus on the ski business and use capital to improve the mountain, not own the asset. Nick, Ian, and I did not want to be in the real estate business, and we didn't have the cash lying around to buy the land anyway. Wolf Mountain (now Canyons Village at Park City) had also become available, but we agreed this was not a property we wished to own, so we turned down this opportunity as well. Up until this point, the ski industry was a fairly small arena, almost like a family, where everyone knew everyone else, and most of us were dutifully dedicated to creating optimal adventures for our customers. Even though we were competitors, we were also friends, and we worked together when we could. Many deals were done with a handshake, and everyone was honest and had similar values. Park City had gained a lot of attention over the years, and it caught the eye of a shrewd real estate developer from Toronto named Jack Bistricer with the Talisker Corporation. No one in the industry had seen the likes of Bistricer before; he was a cutthroat wheeler-dealer with no regard for the shared love of the mountains and their role as the fabric of the community. Reports from Toronto claimed that he was unscrupulous and would sell his mother for the right price. Jack quickly swept in and purchased not only the Park City land but also the land under the Canyons resort from UPCM.

The 2002 Olympics had catapulted Park City to a new level, and we were more focused than ever on KPIs and becoming a top-five resort. Nick and I had worked with a CFO for the past ten years, but he left, and we needed someone new to help manage our costs and our growth initiative. In 2008 we hired a different CFO who brought in her team of people. The auditors continued to remind us that the major risk to our company was the lease management. I was reassured by the new CFO that we had a flagging system in place to make sure we did not miss a lease renewal. I believed that the lease terms were being adequately monitored and handled appropriately. As mentioned, the leases were complicated and some of them were coterminous, and one would trigger another. In 2011, when the flagging system alerted the accounting department it was time to renew, whoever was doing the paperwork renewed the leases in the wrong order. They discovered the problem a few weeks later and rectified it, but it resulted in us technically defaulting on the lease agreement. We were alerted to the issue at a board meeting later that year, but to our knowledge, Talisker had never acknowledged or noticed that we were late with the renewal. We all agreed that the best thing to do was be a transparent and honest partner, so we wrote a letter to clarify the situation and make sure that they had received the leases. I scheduled a meeting with Jack in Toronto to discuss the situation. At first, he played it cool and said he understood it was a clerical error and he didn't want to fight about things, but technically we were in default, and he wanted to negotiate a new lease. As one might imagine, the new lease was not at all favorable for PCMR. Jack was a businessman and a developer; I was part of the ski industry and wanted to make a better mountain. Our goals and values were at odds. He wanted us to do all the work while he made all the money. During one of our first meetings, he asked if I knew who his wife was. When I indicated that I did not, he said tersely, "You should look her up." He wanted me to know that his wife was part of the family that owned De Beers diamond company and that I should be intimidated by their wealth and power.

Jack's position was that since he owned the land, then he owned the resort. However, POWDR owned the base facilities and the parking lots. Jack told me good luck in running a ski resort without ski terrain, and I told him good luck running a ski resort without parking or ski lifts and facilities. And so it went.

"I know you want to be a mountain big shot, maybe you can work for me?" he offered. Jack would often lie to me, and I could tell because as he was talking, he would rub the top of his head and look over my right shoulder as he spoke. I would return from these encounters feeling like a popped balloon. There was just no way to negotiate with the guy. In one of the many meetings I had with Ian and David, my father said, "This is going to get difficult."

"I am so sorry; I hope I can make it up to you guys. I am bereft." I said as I crumpled into one of the office chairs.

Dad put his chin in his hands and responded, "You don't write the check for the rent, shit happens, we will deal with it." His "onward" stoicism led the way.

We were at an impasse and decided to appeal to the courts. Since the ski resort was at the heart of the community, the local courts could intercede and mediate a new lease because a negative result would have a huge, nearly unrecoverable economic impact on the greater community. There was some precedence in the country (mostly in blue states) where this had happened. We knew it was a long shot since we were in a relatively conservative state, but it was the only avenue available to us other than closing the resort.

My father, being the reliable capitalist that he was, concluded that the only way to win was to call their bluff and close the mountain. Objectively speaking, this was the right thing to do. Ian was transaction-oriented; he bought cheap and sold high, but I was an operator. I was polishing the gem, and I was in the business to be enduring. This was not truffle hunting.

My belly filled with fire as I exploded, "No way, and you are not going to say that out loud ever again." Ian saw my conviction, heard the intensity in my tone, and he backed down. He understood my concern for the community and the common good, our family's position within that community, and my reputation. My willingness to preserve the mountain took precedence over "winning," and we never argued about it after the initial conversation. And besides, he was a sucker for conviction!

Jack Bistricer wasn't inclined to deal with an extended lawsuit, so he went to Rob Katz, the chairman and chief executive of Vail Resorts as well as a longtime frenemy of mine and offered to sell him the PCMR land and the Canyons. Rob immediately seized on the opportunity. When I heard this, I knew we were going to lose. I attempted to negotiate with Rob but to no avail, he would not sell us the land or renegotiate the lease. Vail is a large company with deep pockets, and Rob knew he had me by the balls. Hell, everyone knew it. At that point, I decided to do as well as I could while knowing that in the end, I was going to be defeated. I wanted to make it hurt less, so we threw everything we had at the situation, and we continued to push the case up through the court system; every month we could keep the mountain open we would continue to employ people in the community, maintain our level of service, and take as much cash out of the business as possible. It was my obligation to create the best result possible for all our shareholders, and this was the only path available to us. I hold no ill will towards Rob. I respected and understood his position and the way he negotiated. Bistricer, not so much.

For my family and I, this was probably one of the most horrifying times of our lives, aside from my MS diagnosis. My wife and kids were ostracized, and many times they came home crying. The entire mess was being played out daily in every media source in the state. Dad tried to quell our agony by quoting one of his favorite books, *Gulliver's Travels*, "Don't let the Lilliputians bring you down!" he howled. It was particularly difficult to see the community where I lived, worked, raised my children, and invested time and money turn against us. It was gut-wrenching. I had such purity of intent when I went into this business. I was so excited to own, grow, and improve the ski resort. I loved the damn thing, and I loved the community. I could not believe I was so stupid to have let this happen. And it was hardly about the money, it was everything else. As the leader my father trained me to be, I took full responsibility for the error; I had built this business, I had gained when we were successful, and now I lost when we failed. It was my greatest career debacle, and I did it in front of everyone who mattered to me. I remember saying to my wife and kids as we sat around the dinner table, "Guys, you are going to watch your father fail miserably in front of everyone in town. I'm sorry. But I'm going to fight this until I can't fight anymore. Everyone is going to say I'm a jerk. But they would do the same thing. I hope you would, too. These things happen, it was no one's intent. Watch how I handle myself, and if I don't make you proud then I will change."

For two and a half years this went on, and throughout that time, I was in a near-constant state of fight or flight terror, often with cold sweats, trembling, tears, and crippling self-castigation. I thought back to the time when Dad was battling with Brooke Grant and the toll it took on him and our family. It was part of doing business, but certainly not the part that anyone looks forward to. We went through agonizing depositions, meetings, rulings that were mostly not in our favor, and continued scrutiny in the press and our personal lives. Finally, the judge had enough.

Judge Ryan said, "Either you go to mediation and figure this out, or I will make the decision, and no one will be happy."

He sent us to Colorado Springs to meet with a mediator and come up with an agreement. My father was in the room with us, along with our lawyer, Mike Zimmerman, as well as Rob Katz and his people. Ian was the biggest dog in the room at the time, and I would like to think that Katz was at least a bit intimidated. Our first offer was, of course, rejected. I didn't want to sell it for any amount of money, but we had fought for as long as we could, and we were basically out of options. Katz told me, "At some point, you *will* lose and get evicted." We finally agreed on a price to be acquired by Vail. Financially, it was a win for POWDR. But from an emotional perspective, I was devastated at having lost the property where my career began. The resort that Nick had groomed into being, the place where my kids had grown up skiing. If I hadn't been in a room full of lawyers and CEOs, I would have let out a strangled sob. When we reported to the board, there was silence in the room. It was broken by Dave McKown, who simply stated, "It was manna from heaven, we will never mention it again." The deal was good for our bottom line, but it had happened in such a way that we all wanted to put it in the past and not speak of it again.

Of course, I did reflect on the incident and try to learn from it. POWDR survived, and we grew in our expertise and our strength. We still want to provide the best guest impression, but that goal has to be filtered through what is best for the company as a whole. I became less focused on KPIs and more intent on hiring the best possible people to run POWDR. The next CFO I hired I interviewed five times, to the point of almost being ridiculous. He propped us up and helped get us through that time after the lawsuit and move ahead in our operations and further acquisitions. He is now CEO of POWDR. The lawsuit and the aftermath softened me a bit. When POWDR goes into a community, we try to explain ourselves. Communication is key to facilitating a smooth transition. In the words of Nick Badami, mountains are community gems, and you must show them the respect they deserve. In a way they are like sports teams—everyone believes they have a stake in their future, and we have a responsibility to all our shareholders to create an enduring asset. We feel privileged to be part of the community ecosystem, and if you give a little bit of love, you get a lot more back. There will inevitably be disagreements, but if you treat people amicably, that karma goes a long way. If we do our jobs well, everyone on and around the mountain should prosper.

Play Forever

My brother David and I learned a great deal about philanthropy from our father but have also worked to devise our strategy. David, in his role as the Chair of the Cumming Foundation, aims to fund solutions to the root cause of a problem as well as invest in projects that move the dial significantly. We apply Ian's axiom of "never investing in a business that we didn't understand" to the charities we work with. The Cumming Foundation exhaustively researches each issue and brings what is needed to a particular market in a way that will have the most impact. As a family foundation, we endeavor to use Dad's principles to have an enduring influence as we continue to live up to our responsibility.

At POWDR, we created *Play Forever*—a philanthropic program that is committed to protecting and enhancing the mountain towns in which so many people love to work, live, and play. We sometimes refer to the mountain town as a bubble—it is an amazing environment where people live a lifestyle that they choose, in a place that they choose, among others with similar values in a beautiful mountain setting. Both Nick and my father instilled in me the importance of leaving my community a better place than I found it, and they ingrained in me a responsibility to pay it forward whenever possible. We have deep compassion for the towns where we want to *Play Forever*, and as part of this philanthropic commitment, we established community foundations in each of the communities where we have businesses. The foundations are in touch with what each community needs to thrive and can expertly distribute funds where they are needed the most, and in a more informed way than a larger umbrella foundation could.

Canaries in a Coal Mine

Thirty years after my dad planted trees to offset his footprint, and got involved with the Nature Conservancy, the climate problem has only gotten progressively worse. Being in the ski industry for the last three decades we have been able to see first-hand the impacts of global warming in our diminished snowfall, lower watersheds, droughts, etc. We, along with coastal communities and island nations, are the proverbial canaries in the coal mine, as our friends at the Aspen Ski Company coined it years ago. We will feel the force of nature before the rest of the population. Ian planted trees and saved the land from development, but POWDR has been able to take environmental activism to the next level by using the latest technology available to us.

Unlike other global problems, the answers to slowing climate change are available and attainable. We have the science and technology within our reach that can save the planet. What we are missing is the impetus for *everyone* to get involved at a mass level. After I talked to some people who helped and inspired me, my thoughts solidified into actions that I felt I could take as an individual, and through POWDR, to address climate change in some tiny way. The ski industry uses a lot of power, and when we improve the mountain for our customers, it can tear up the slopes. But we continue to do the best we can within the confines of our reality to mitigate our carbon footprint. POWDR resorts have applied a variety of resources to change our power consumption for the better, including altering traffic patterns, buying cow power, utilizing solar panels, buying wind offsets, protecting watersheds, mitigating runoff, employing tier four snowcats, installing triple pane windows, and adding modern co-generation at some of our resorts. These improvements have resulted in a 50% reduction in our carbon footprint thus far. We have added solar and wind energy and biofuels to each one of our properties. To date, we have been involved with Save Our Snow, 1% for Nature, and Protect Our Winters (POW), to name a few. The Woodward facility in Park City features a roof that is two-thirds solar and one-third living. Each of the POWDR properties has a green team, and we have a corporate VP whose primary job is to oversee our green policies and manage our carbon footprint. Using knowledge from the climbing world, I believe we need to prepare for the worst while hoping for the best.

The Bird

As the story is told, Ted Johnson was the "founder" of Snowbird ski resort, Dick Bass was the "funder," and Ian was the "finisher." When Dick Bass bought Snowbird, he decided that it would be his enduring legacy to the world. He was from oil country and possessed an oversized Texas personality that dominated most conversations, he always told anyone who would listen, in his husky Texan accent, "Snowbird is the best place in the world to nurture mind, body, and spirit." He loved to talk and tell stories about his days as a climber, which were impressive. He was the first American climber to scale the highest peak on each of the seven continents and for a time was the oldest to summit Mt.

Everest—he had my admiration and respect from the very beginning. Dick and Ian had a similar magnetism—both were charismatic, larger-than-life people, both had a touch of ADD (attention deficit disorder), and both were successful businessmen. Because Ian was a regular at Snowbird, they knew each other and had a kind of "frenemy" relationship. It is common knowledge that developing the resort over the years almost bankrupted Dick, who once told me, "I never knew how rich I was until I wasn't." Dad would jokingly ask every year or so, "When are you going to sell me this place?" And Dick would laugh and retort in his breathless Texas drawl, "Now dammit Ian you know that ain't gonna happen!"

For Ian, as we know, capital was always king. He was able to spot a valuable, irreplaceable asset, as well as any mismanagement or broken aspects that would suggest unrealized value. During the 1980s, Ian had also become an expert at buying distressed debt, and there was a lot of it around. Meanwhile, Dick Bass had amazing visions for what he wanted Snowbird to be, but he was chronically overborrowing, and sometimes the notes were sold at a discount and put into the resolution trust corporation for distressed debt (RTC). Ian became aware of this fact and tried to buy the Snowbird debt from RTC. Dick got wind of his efforts and felt betrayed. It created a kink in their relationship, but they remained frenemies. Again, for Ian, he was just playing full-contact capitalism.

Dick continued riding out the highs and lows of the ski resort business, alternating between accumulating debt, making valuable improvements in Snowbird, and being on the brink of bankruptcy, only to rise like a phoenix over and over again. Somehow, over forty-three years, he kept things going and retained control. Like Dad and I, Dick had a stubborn entrepreneurial spirit, and he was 100% focused on his passion for fulfilling Snowbird's vast potential. His management style was controversial; he would randomly hire some guy he met on a plane to run the resort, or he would haphazardly fire employees. One time, to keep funding Snowbird's expansion efforts, he ended up selling Ian the "Snowbird house," the only single-family home in Snowbird at the time—right across from the resort. It is an architectural statement piece, built into the side of the mountain like something out of a James Bond movie. Another time, Dick sold Ian a chunk of shares in Alta to raise money to fund his efforts. Because of the amount of time we spent at Snowbird, and our father's ever-increasing share in the mountain, we truly felt like we were part of the community. More than that, we were infatuated with it almost as much as Dick was.

Harry Whittington, Bass's friend, and longtime lawyer described Dick as "An epic Texan, filled with unbridled enthusiasm and perfection, everything he did was complete. He didn't leave anything unfinished. He just ran out of time on some things." In 2012, Dick was diagnosed with pulmonary fibrosis, and he found himself in a problematic situation where he had not set up Snowbird within his estate in a way that would allow him to pass it down to his children, and it was, by far, his largest asset. Moreover, none of his kids had an interest in running the mountain. Because of my own experience with illness, I often reach out to others who are diagnosed with chronic conditions, so I got in touch with Dick. We agreed to meet for lunch, which started at noon, and as often was the case when dealing with Dick, the meeting lasted through cocktail hour. He explained his predicament and said that he wanted to entrust Snowbird to someone who would love and take care of it. I told him that POWDR would love to buy Snowbird, but his COO at the time, Bob Bonar, was not in favor of this plan. He had heard about some of our acquisitions (i.e., Killington) and that we had been negligent in our communications (though not our efforts), and he was concerned. Also, during this period, POWDR had not resolved the PCMR lawsuit, so our balance sheet probably would not allow us to obtain a loan to buy Snowbird.

Consequently, it was decided that Ian should be the one to purchase Snowbird. Dick's opening offer was almost twenty times EBITDA (earnings before interest, taxes, depreciation, and amortization), and Ian responded with an offer that was closer to five times EBITDA. The deal was going nowhere until Snowbird's CFO at the time, Tom Jones, bridged the gap and got the deal back on track. Dick then proposed a more fair-minded figure that was ten times EBITDA, which at the time, was more than full retail. Ian had been a value investor throughout his entire career; he had never paid full retail for any asset in his life, even for Kermit the Gulfstream! He called me, ranting, "It is not worth more than eight times EBITDA tops, that fucking loudmouth Texan is crazy!" His financial advisors at the family office were not supportive of the acquisition; we were already heavily invested in the ski industry, so it wouldn't help us diversify much. Ian had accumulated his wealth and power with the spots of a value investor, and he had a hard time shaking them off at this point in his life.

"Dad," I paused for effect, "We grew up here. Everything we've ever done together started here, you've wanted it for over forty years, why are you even debating this? You will never get Snowbird for less than he's asking. The demand for the Snowbird experience is so high now and in the future that the resort can't possibly meet it. You will never lose money." Dad wasn't used to the subjective weighing so heavily in an investment decision. Objectively, it was probably not the best buy, but in his heart, he couldn't pass it up. He was so used to being objective-minded and not paying retail that he needed to be able to blame someone else for violating his principles. While I would like to think he was calling me for advice, I believe he knew that he was going to do the deal, but he didn't want to be solely responsible for the decision.

For me, during the most trying time of my career, knowing that Snowbird would always be a part of our family was a huge consolation prize. I was utterly overwhelmed by the embarrassment and sheer mess of navigating the lawsuit with PCMR and Vail and the toll it was taking on my family. The prospect of the Snowbird transaction restored my hope and energy. Bob Bonar performed shuttle diplomacy between Dick and Dad, and when he announced that Dick was going to sign the deal, I burst into tears from both relief and happiness. Snowbird rivals any of the most celebrated mountains around the world, and our family was going to own it. The wide range of terrain, the extensive number of bowls, the stunning vistas, the light powdery snow, and the unbelievable blue-sky days make it idyllic. When you add to that our family history, it is, in fact, irreplaceable. While I was sad that POWDR wouldn't be the one signing this dream deal, it was a true solace that Snowbird would be with us, hopefully in perpetuity. It gave my heart something else to love and cherish. Many people thought that we would be absentee owners, but we were determined to make Snowbird the best version of itself. We had learned from our mistakes with other acquisitions, and the Snowbird integration would be done more masterfully.

The closing took place at the Seven Summits club under the bridge, and Dick, once a powerful climber, arrived in a wheelchair due to the progression of his illness. It was important to Dick that he passed the baton to a family that would continue his legacy of love and sustaining the mountain. A family who cherished its dramatic peaks, as well as its community feel. In the end, Dad said to Dick, "Snowbird is an heirloom, not an asset, and we will treat it as such." It was the last time that Dick would be at Snowbird, and there was a stoic finality to the moment.

The Fulcrum

The fulcrum has been a driving force in my life. It is the symbol of what I do. The POWDR logo is a fulcrum, and it implies balance. For me, it is the ultimate goal. What principles and values do we apply to our decision-making and why? Whatever position or action we take must be motivated and constructed with balance in mind. We apply these principles in our work, our relationships, parenting, marriage, friendships, and community. Finding a way to balance the objective and subjective has been integral to my life's work, and it is continually evolving. Work/life balance. The balance between protecting the environment and promoting progress. The balance between managing my health while still doing the things I love. The balance of power between me and my father. The balance of being a successful capitalist while preserving the common good. The balance between creating profitable, enduring properties while nurturing the communities where they dwell. The balance of continuing the climb with the need to preserve energy for the trickier descent. It all comes down to making judgments and applying principles in a way that keeps things in balance. In making these judgments, am I being a good father, citizen, steward, and partner? I feel like my father was often out of balance in terms of his life and his work, and much of what I do and why I do it is a reaction to his choices. Being in the mountains was life-enhancing for me, and I want to bring that feeling to others. Everything I do supports this goal, but always within the context of maintaining balance.

My family is in the outdoor business for a reason—because we are passionate about protecting and boosting our communities and the adventure lifestyle so that people can be active in the outdoors, challenge themselves, learn new tricks, and have fun doing the things they love with the people they love. At a philosophical level, it's about giving people the chance to develop as healthy human beings through engagement with nature. I have had this calling since I was a boy skiing at Snowbird with my family, and it was made stronger as I climbed as a young man. It is my goal to adhere to this vision and these values, which brought us to where we are today.

Reflected Light

Dad's experience with his parents and the meandering start to his professional career influenced his parenting style. He encouraged us to follow our path and "march to the beat of your own drummer." That was easier said than done, given Ian's iconic businessman status. His friends and co-workers occasionally approached us and said, "I know your father; he is quite a man." This statement was always flattering but also intimidating. Growing up as the son of someone like that could feel a little emasculating at times—we got some reflected light, but we mostly got shade because he was such a tall tree.

Dad had a way of providing subtle, manipulative encouragement. When I was a boy, he would point at me and say, "You, John Cumming, can do anything you set your mind to." I'm sure other parents have said this to their kids, but to me, it didn't feel like a general observation. It felt prophetic. There was an intention behind the statement that put a point on the horizon for me. His mere suggestion made me stretch to reach that point. He never doubted that I was capable, so I didn't either. I believe if he had said, "Just do your best," it would have provided me with an escape. When we were on the Grand Teton, he genuinely believed I could climb that rock at eleven years old. Of course, it was scary, it hurt, and it was traumatic at the time, but I accepted it and learned from the experience. It served a purpose in my life: to create resilience and pain tolerance. When I had to go in front of the judge and choose between my parents, I did what was asked of me. At Snowbird with my brother, we defied the odds and made it down the master ski run in Scott's bowl. Later, when he cut me off after flunking at Boulder, I found a path forward as a mountain climber. Every time I faced a challenge, Ian knew I would figure it out. So, when it was time for me to start my own business, he had faith in me. Dad had seen firsthand my ability to persevere. He always believed in the tough old boot part of my personality, and he fostered it in many ways (some admittedly unconventional). Facing and overcoming a myriad of obstacles as a young man also allowed me to endure my chronic health condition.

Ian had an inspiring vitality about him that made many people, not just me, want to live up to what he thought of them to please him. I was a classic underachiever in academia, and now I'm an overachiever—and I blame it on him! Ian's absence made me hungry. His affirmation made me strive. And his attention made me grateful. And without those three things, I don't think I would be where I am today.

Ian was unapologetically himself in all walks of life—as a business leader, friend, father, and grandfather. I didn't realize what a great parent he was or what a terrible parent he was until I was a parent myself. I made sure to be more present for my kids' experiences than my dad. And thanks to him, I was able to make the deliberate choice to be present with my children. We all screw our kids up in ways we can't see or foresee. In some ways, Dad's absence might have served me well, and my being around my kids so much might not be an advantage in the long run. Maybe they will be sick of me or not as self-reliant as I had to be, but they will balance it in their own way.

Ian loved and supported his grandchildren, but he wasn't the type of grandpa to get down on the ground and play games with them; he was a businessman until the very end. He didn't soften up and become a diaper-changing, hands-on grandfather, but he watched them play from his office, and he loved to cheer them on in their various endeavors. I remember him watching our daughter, Quinn, perform the role of Clara in the Ballet West production of *The Nutcracker* in Park City with tears streaming down his face. He had been a long-time supporter of the ballet and had paid for her dance lessons. She said of her grandfather, "He was my biggest fan, the most supportive grandparent I ever had. He was very real. Many people in his business can be stuck up and snobby, but he wasn't. He was a force to be reckoned with, and he inspired me. I miss him." Our other daughter, Carina, recalls getting big hugs from her grandfather, and her face would be stuffed into his belly. "He always talked to me like an adult, never a child, which felt cool and empowering. He would also break into these crazy little songs that he had made up (his sense of humor was not safe for children), along with a dance that made us laugh. Sometimes, he would give me $100!" And his grandson, Shane, had this to say about Ian, "My grandfather was, of course, a legendary philanthropist and businessman, but to me, he was just Grandpa Ian. I didn't fully understand his impact on the world until after he passed, but it was clear his influence on me had broader implications. Ian was always curious, which made me feel like he was genuinely interested in my passions, struggles, and questions. He also treated everyone he met with equal respect, easily connecting with people from all walks of life, a skill I greatly admire. Finally, he was relentless in all his endeavors. The idea of giving up was never an option, and I felt this every time I was around my grandpa. It is no wonder the kid from Saskatchewan found such success in his life."

Onward!

The Hungry Ghost

The hungry ghost is a philosophical concept derived from Buddhism that describes "beings who are driven by intense emotional needs in an animalistic way." It is depicted as a creature with a huge tooth-lined mouth, a distended belly, and a long pencil-thin throat that prevents the belly from ever being filled.[7] I explored this idea with my father many times over the years starting when I was in middle school, as I watched him make sacrifices with his family and relationships to create more capital and gather wealth. After his marriage to Bobbie ended, my brother and I spent a lot of time with our nanny while he traveled and worked, and I finally asked him, *how much is enough, what is the end game?* His response never wavered throughout his life, *"More."*

When Dad was perplexed and working through something, he would go into this trance-like existence, almost catatonic. His leg would bounce, and he would move his head around almost like he was having

---

[7] Description from Mike Zimmerman

a dialogue with someone. Even if we were in the same room with him, he was absent. I would try to talk to him, and he would stare out the window and not respond. My brother and I would physically grab him and say, "What are you speeching about?" Meaning, what are you so lost in thought about that you can't be present with us at this moment?

As I got older and learned more about his upbringing, I came to understand that capitalism was his way of rebalancing the karma from his past—the abandonment of his biological father, the distance he felt from his adoptive father, and the criticism from his mother. He was so driven by the challenge, the neurosis, the attainment that he couldn't even enunciate why he kept going—why he needed "more." A hungry ghost is constantly seeking something outside itself to curb an insatiable yearning for relief or fulfillment. The validation Ian received from his work was like a drug filling his needs, and his self-worth was reflected in his wealth and power. He wouldn't or perhaps couldn't stop to weigh the cost of this addiction on his family life. Maybe it was his ADHD that wouldn't allow him to fully reflect on this in a meaningful way or perhaps he was still running from the judgment he felt as a child. He would often say, "I can't figure out how to get off the bus," or "I've got the tiger by the tail, but I can't let it go." He knew he was on a volatile ride and that he would have to make many sometimes painful sacrifices, but like a quintessential hungry ghost, he couldn't stop.

I asked Dad again when I was a young adult, "Why do you need this?" He looked at me with very serious eyes and said, "Whatever you do, don't follow in my footsteps because I am crazy." At some level, he knew he couldn't control his incessant need to be successful and wealthy. That need was a core part of him and drove him at the most fundamental level. While I saw the effect his laser focus had on his life and experienced the sacrifices first-hand, this was the only role model that I had growing up. My father was trying to *prove himself* and validate his existence, and I did the same because I was seeking to *prove myself to him*. The way to get into his orbit was to be a businessman. While I've never loved anyone more than my father, I also never resented anyone more. Both things will probably be true of my children with me. How do we value ourselves and the people that we love? Ian considered a "serious person" someone who was smart enough to see the opportunity, talented enough to take advantage of it, and focused enough to succeed. If you could do all these things, then he would help you. When I created my business, Ian sensed I had the "capitalist gene," and he offered his guidance and help. To me, that mentorship represented love and closeness, and it drew me forward. I wanted to be near him, and capitalism was the path to get there. When I was growing my business, I would call him for help, and he would offer, "Oof, that's a tough one, this is masters level stuff, here is what I would do," and we would proceed to have a wonderful dialogue. Later, I would call, and he would say, "Look, John, I've got my own problems; go figure it out." As he got older, he relinquished the expert role a bit. He would say, "John, I have no idea. You are better at this stuff than me." Such was the arc of our father/son journey.

About fifteen years ago, I realized I was making significant sacrifices—to my family, health, and community. Although Dad didn't waste time reflecting on some of these things, I couldn't stop thinking about them, and I owned them in a way that Ian never did. Yet I kept compulsively doing it—acquiring more, growing the business more. Even as I struggled with my health and its effect on my life and my family, I kept plugging away because that is what I watched my father do; it replaced the feeling of achievement I was used to getting from my physical accomplishments. Our values and our paths were different. Dad was an entrepreneur in an investment way, and I was an entrepreneur in the more traditional sense. Dad built his business primarily by focusing on the objective, while I built my business by focusing on the subjective value that our resorts bring to people. Dad wasn't cognizant of his sacrifices, but I was hyper-focused on them. Nevertheless, we both wound up in the same situation. Neither of us needed more money or validation at a certain point, but we couldn't get off the bus. We were both addicted to the thrill of the next adventure, the next brass ring. Predictably, I had mapped my self-worth to the same set of values that I had been questioning my father about for thirty years. As I reflect on the cumulative experiences I have under my belt as a leader and a human, I can better understand some of my father's decisions and priorities that I challenged when I was younger.

All capitalists climb a hill of fear; the higher up the hill they get, the more they feel the exposure. There are too many relationships and experiences to monitor, and as they ascend the mountain there comes a point where there is more to lose than there is to gain. And so, we must decide—do we live to climb another day, or do we need to summit every time? At POWDR, several thousand people work for a business that gives them objective and subjective compensation, and we have exchanged commitments. I can't suddenly pretend that those commitments don't exist, and those people have not invested their faith in our organization. It is not just about me anymore; everyone involved has something to lose as we climb the mountain together, and like any climb, there are complicated choices that need to be made for the good of the team and, in the case of POWDR, the whole company.

When my father was close to retirement, he reveled in tutoring others and allowing them a chance to succeed, even when it wasn't how he would have done it. At this point in my career, I am ready to take on more of a rocket booster role. I want to share my experiences, and I look forward to being able to catapult my family. I am not a rocket anymore, but I still have enough fuel to help mentor and boost my family and friends if asked. As long as they are engaged in the career or activity they choose, I will do whatever I can to propel them forward.

Courage!

Several times throughout my life when I was going through rough patches, I would receive a handwritten note from Dad (on his personalized stationery "from the desk of Ian Cumming") that said just one word. **Courage!** This was exceedingly powerful and useful to me. Implied in his message was motivation: you can do this, keep going, and this too shall pass! He emboldened me to champion and defend my beliefs, to be self-confident, to demonstrate conviction, and to have the willingness to battle with the world until it took the shape I wanted. "If the world doesn't yield to your wishes, beat on it until it does." Was one of Ian's favorite adages. Just as important as his little reminders was the precedent he set as a human being.

Dad was a warrior—he always fought for what he believed in, he had a high tolerance for uncertainty, and he was willing to take on responsibility, share success, and fail publicly. He dealt with the illness that finally took him with the same level of courage, grace, and grit that he exemplified throughout his life. When he was diagnosed with mild cognitive impairment (MCI), he was still the master of his universe—wealthy, powerful, and self-assured.

One afternoon, we sat together on the idyllic back porch of his home in East Hampton, where we had shared so many wonderful memories. The porch wrapped around the entire house, and roomy rocking chairs painted bright white sat amongst flower boxes filled with brightly colored geraniums. Immediately in front of us was the tree swing where my children had played with their cousins when they were younger. A vast expanse of kelly-green lawn reached the peaceful allure of Hook Pond, and beyond that, the illustrious Maidstone golf course. It was one of his favorite places in the world, and he had worked tirelessly to acquire the very setting we now enjoyed. As we sat there quietly, he finally said, "One of the most difficult things about this is that one of these days I'm going to be sitting here in this amazing place, looking at this view, and not knowing what the hell I'm looking at."

Ian's decline started, and it became more evident with every passing day. His combatant tendencies came out in full force—he was fighting the disease, fighting with Joe over his leadership role at Leucadia, and fighting with the board. Jay Nichols, who had been on the board at Leucadia since its inception and had known Ian since high school, did not recognize Ian's deterioration at first. He was still so funny, and his character was so strong, that he could wield his power to convince people of his point, even though his words were jumbled. But Joe certainly noticed, and he was pressuring Ian to step down. Finally, we had a difficult conversation where I said, "I admire your tenacity and I understand that you are battling to retain what you built, but I don't think the acrimony and frustration are helping your health." Selfishly, I wanted to protect and preserve him for as long as I could. He asked me what I wanted him to do, and I told him that I thought he should resign and that maybe it was time to shift his focus to building the family office. The power dynamics had forever changed at Leucadia, and he accepted it with grace and courage; he surrendered his sword and did what was asked of him.

The brain, like the immune system, can also be viewed like an onion. The brain has layers, beginning at the core with early memories and instincts, and as you create more experiences and learn more, the onion thickens with knowledge and memory. With an Alzheimer's diagnosis, the layers of the onion start to wither, and they dry up and eventually fall away. The drying process can seem random and unpredictable, but the core of the onion is usually still there. While Ian's recall and cognitive function declined, his core attributes became more pronounced; he was affectionate, humorous, lighthearted, and appreciative of his relationships. The shrewd, intellectual side of the Raven was fading away, but his playful side shone through. As the illness progressed, Dad did his best to stay in his sweet spot. Even though he knew he would lose and that we were watching, he was resolute in his effort to keep going forward. "Onward!" he would always say. He got up every day, put on his suit, and went to the office—it was truly inspiring. As time went by, he didn't need as much courage to get through his days because his mind was leaving him. It was harder for the people around him at that point; we needed the strength to accept this new version of Ian.

Dad had been by my side during many years of dealing with my health struggles, and I was right there for him throughout his testing, helping him navigate the best course of action, once again with the expert and thoughtful advice from Dr. Henry McFarland. Ian was a good sport about everything. He willingly had the tests done and met with doctors and received experimental treatments, and all the time he never seemed unhappy or worried. Unfortunately, the outcome for people with Alzheimer's is not positive, even though we tried our best to improve Ian's outcome. When people ask me about the process, I remind them that it is an exceedingly long journey full of peaks and valleys where sometimes you see glimpses of this person and you want to believe so badly that they are there with you, and just as quickly they are gone. It is a battlefield of emotion, without the hope of victory, but I still let myself invest my emotions in the hope and expectation that we could crack this nut, too. MS and Alzheimer's are not comparable; an MCI diagnosis almost always results in Alzheimer's or dementia, and the therapies are not there yet to cure or even abate the disease. It was devastating to me that I could not help him as he had helped me. As the disease ate away at Dad's brain, we would take notice and commiserate together as a family, acknowledging that we were losing our father/friend/husband as we knew him. Yet, there would still be times when he would appear to be his old self, and we would be deluded into thinking that he was fine, that maybe this diagnosis was incorrect, or he would somehow beat the odds and the last few months were just a bad dream. Then his symptoms would resurface the next day, and I would go through the whole mourning process again. It was draining, and a waste of time.

In retrospect, I wish in many ways that I had been more thoughtful of the moments we had together and accepting of his disease and the person he had become. I regret that I didn't spend more time just being with him—without judgment, resentment, or striving for a different result. Forgiving him and forgiving myself. It is easy to say, but hard to act on. He was content, it was the rest of us who needed to accept the new relationship we had with him. It was so important to us, his family, that he stay alive, and outwardly he seemed accepting of our efforts. He would sometimes ask me to put a bottle of whiskey near his bed in case he decided to go outside one night and let nature take its course. Over time, he got beyond the point of caring, he was so disassociated from reality that he didn't know whether he was hungry or cold, and his mind would forget to take care of his body. But he always knew who we were, David, Annette, and I—right up until the day he died. We were grateful for that.

My brother and I had been taking turns each week having dinner with Ian and were both spending as much time with him as possible. One day my brother called and said, "Have you spoken to your father lately?" (This was a joke we had of referring to him as the other's father.) "I had a pretty weird experience with him, and I think things are progressing quickly." I assured David that I would check it out. My first call was to Annette to determine whether she had also noticed a further downward slide, and she confirmed that she had. I called Dad and proposed that we go to our house in Solana Beach for dinner and spend time together that week. He agreed, and I picked him up in Jackson. During our flight, I quickly realized that something had changed. He had been communicating in sentence fragments for a while, but he was still articulate enough and used hand gestures, so you could usually figure out what he was saying. During this visit, he started using vocal noises and tones instead of words to communicate. He was cooing like a baby and making a warble type of sound, kind of like a meadowlark. He was perfectly cheerful, and he looked much the same as he always did, but it was like he was an infant. I had been seeing him every week, so it was startling to see such a rapid and astounding regression. Yet, he seemed happy to be with me, and content to be sitting around the fire having a cocktail.

Around 9:00 p.m., he looked at me and exclaimed, "Night Night!"

I helped put him to bed in the master bedroom, and then went back out to the deck and sat quietly by myself, listening to the waves crash against the sand, the moonlight lingering across the water like an exclamation point. This moment, which I knew had been coming for quite some time, was upon me, and still, I was unprepared for it. I numbed myself by polishing off the rest of the bottle of vodka, and I finally got to sleep sometime after midnight. The next morning, I awoke, bleary-eyed in our girls' bedroom at 6:15 a.m. to see my dad with the sun shining brightly behind him, fully dressed with his shirt slightly untucked, big bright eyes, his briefcase and suitcase in hand, asking, "What's next?"

I replied, "Next, we go down and get a cup of coffee."

I called my brother and said, "I think you're right. I think he's gone."

Shortly thereafter, he was committed to the hospital. His valet and chef, Wayne, helped get him there. Dad was feisty, and defiant, and clearly wanted to leave. He ran down the hallway, naked under his hospital gown, yelling, "Wayne, let's go!" Wayne did his best to deter him and physically keep him at the hospital, while Ian bellowed, "WAYNE YOU PUSSY!"

Near the end, specialists in neuroscience, department heads of neurology, and even the chief medical officer gathered around Dad's bed to deliberate what to try next. He couldn't walk or talk, and he hadn't eaten for quite a while. None of us wanted him to go, but he was certain; he had fought his fate and wished it to end. Finally, he raised his hand and pointed at the sky, and the message was obvious, "I'm done fighting. Let me go." This was a clear signal that now it was time for those around him to be courageous and make the difficult but poignant decision to let him die. Annette, David, and I knew that he was ready to take his last breath in peace at home, in Jackson Hole, looking out at the Tetons surrounded by his family, and we needed to make that happen. Ian lived and died with great courage, and then he gave us the courage to let him go.

We were fortunate to be able to fly him to Jackson Hole on his private jet but getting a heavy-set man who could not walk on and off the plane presented some challenging logistics. Wayne was there waiting for us at the hospital, and he helped us get him into the car. Then we drove to the airport. When we got there, David, Wayne, and I looked at each other and then at Ian, who had one leg that wouldn't bend and seemed to be frothing at the mouth. We were perplexed as to how the three of us would be able to hoist him up the stairs to the plane. David, who is a big strong dude, said to us, "I got it." Then he said to Dad, "Alright buddy, we're going." Wayne and I each seized a leg and David picked Dad up by the torso in a bear hug. Dad's legs were sprawling, David manhandled him to the stairs, and Wayne and I juggled his legs. When we finally got on the plane, David picked Ian up on his own, but this time they were face-to-face as David tried to lift him into the seat. Suddenly, David started crying out in pain because Dad had begun chewing on his neck. I quickly snatched a pillow and wedged it between Dad's teeth and David's neck. David tried to pick him up again, but in a fit of superhuman strength and agility that defied his condition, Ian reached out and violently grabbed David by the balls, and in a perfectly lucid voice shouted, "PUT ME DOWN YOU FUCKER!" It was disturbing, hilarious, and tremendously sad all at the same time.

Even in his last moments, Dad did things the way he wanted. It was his choice to die at home with the early morning light forming an alpenglow on the Grand when the only people in the room were his sons, his wife, and his dog, Claire. I had said my goodbyes before then, but that morning as we were listening for his last breath, I had this weird instinct to lean over the retaining gate of his hospital bed and touch my forehead to his. At the same time, David was also leaning in to hold his hand. The weight of us collapsed the gate, and we both fell into Dad, and he and I ended up cracking heads. The irony and pure metaphysics of the situation was astounding. When at last my dad had found peace, we butted heads for the last time. I like to think that he finally lighted on the summit of the Grand Teton in the form of a raven, looking down at me with a triumphant smile on his face.

When Ian passed away, much like the rest of his life, he didn't want any fanfare. "Ashes to ashes," he would say. But we could not let such a magnanimous soul depart the world without some recognition and celebration of his many achievements. We wanted to strike the right balance of being in a place that we all cherished as a family, without an excess of people or pageantry, something that befitted the impact that Ian had on us and the rest of the world while maintaining his privacy; you couldn't just sprinkle Ian among some wildflowers. We were brainstorming with some of our trusted advisors, one of whom was Dave Fields, the GM of Snowbird. We had decided on Snowbird as the location for the memorial service; it was a place he owned and wanted to share with his children, grandchildren, and great-grandchildren, and it was the mountain he loved the most. It was Dave's idea to put Ian's ashes in the ava-launcher. We quickly adopted the idea. What better way to give Ian the explosive ending he deserved than by shooting him out of a cannon? Especially given his love of the potato launcher back in the day. But there was a hitch—it could be borderline illegal. Avalanche rounds are controlled by federal statute and taking the explosives out and putting ashes in was in a grey area.

Another one of those trusted advisors was Mongo. I met Mongo when I was ten years old when he taught me how to ski powder. He served two tours in Vietnam back as an infantry guy, and Mongo was his call sign. When Snowbird and Alta were developing their avalanche control protocols with the Utah Department of Transportation, Mongo and a few others organized the procedures, storage, and deployment, in keeping with federal and state ordinances. The guys who run these operations in the mountains have military-grade training and are experienced in the deployment of explosives. The ava-launcher is basically a portable military weapon used to launch explosive shells. The idea was to take the explosives out of a few of the shells, replace the gunpowder with Ian's ashes, and then shoot them onto Old Reliable on Twin Peaks. It was so perfect for Ian—somewhat subversive, but also a bit audacious. Mongo was put in charge of the operation. I was always impressed with his presence; he was reassuring and confident, but also kind. Over the years we had stayed in touch, played some golf, and periodically had a couple of drinks together. He quietly took charge of everything. He prepared the warheads with the ashes, programmed the coordinates, etc. We never saw him, he was always behind the scenes, but he executed Dave Fields' fabulous idea.

We planned the memorial for April of 2018 in the Hidden Peak at the Summit Restaurant at Snowbird. It would be by invitation only, and everyone had to take the tram to get there. David, Annette, and I gave eulogies, along with Ian's long-time friend, Bud Scruggs. Then the military operations were executed with perfection; there was a loud explosion and Ian was launched into the universe and landed in the mountain that he so loved and would now forever be a part of. It was at once violent, spectacular, over the top, and fitting for his exit from the world. In a subtle nod to our fallen leader, the Snowbird staff put white angel wings where Ian's ashes landed on the mountain map located in the Tram cars.

My son Shane, only seventeen at the time and named after his grandfather (Ian is Scottish for John, and Shane is the Irish name for John), wanted to play *Blackbird* on acoustic guitar to honor his grandfather. The stage was set for Shane to play at the south end of the building in front of the windows overlooking the Twin Peaks, where we had just exploded his grandfather's ashes. There was rapt silence, and as Shane was playing, a raven began circling him outside the window. Everyone saw it, except Shane, who was intently focused on his music. He missed the supernatural impact the scene was having on the group. The symbolism was astonishing; it was a magical, poignant moment that truly seemed to be a sign from somewhere in the universe.

A couple of months went by, and around the end of June, I got a call in my office at POWDR.

"Hey John, it's Mongo." Pause. "I wanted to know what you want us to do with the rest of your Dad?" He explained, "We couldn't fit him all into three bullets, so I have a zip lock bag here in my desk with the rest of him. Do you want me to bring him to you?"

I had a quiet chuckle before I asked where Mongo was. "I'm at my desk below the lower tram dock."

"Take him up the tram, let him blow into the mineral basin, and please call me when you are done," I instructed.

"Ten-Four." He replied.

About an hour later he called me back, "I think he's happy," he said.

Afterword

Everyone has the desire to know their place in history. With the help of a genealogy company, you can create your family tree by sifting through generations of public records to find the facts—births, deaths, marriages, military service, etc. What happens less of the time and is by far more challenging to excavate are the first-hand descriptions of the people within those family trees. My father generated astonishing power within our family, and I miss his presence, especially his warm hugs, every day. I was motivated by gratitude and love to explore the wisdom that we can gain from his exceptional essence and to make sure that my children, nieces, nephews, and the generation that follows have some record of the magnanimous man who changed the trajectory of our family and our extended community for years to come.

Dad's mother, Granny, as we called her, was an intimidating, matriarchal force in our family. I visited her in Vancouver when she was dying, and she said, "As a life-long atheist, it's really difficult for me to accept the finality of this situation, the diagnosis—the end being the end."

"Granny, I disagree with you. You are immortal," I replied, taking her hand in mine. "The books you've written, your teachings, friendships, and family are there to perpetuate your existence for eternity."

This tribute is my way of immortalizing Ian and preserving his legacy. I hope it has given you a taste of what a wonderfully complex, savory character he was. While enormously successful and generous, he was imperfect: goofy, foul-mouthed, bad-mannered, and infuriatingly resolute. But as we often discover in life, the flaws made him authentic and lovable, and his story worth exploring. His charisma, love, loyalty, optimism, compassion, and ultimately, his humanity are all wired into us, his family, through nature and nurture, and they are immense gifts for which we will always be grateful.

Finally, in my work, I have always shared the triumphs and taken responsibility for the failures, and this is no different. All errors, omissions, or date discrepancies are my own.

Acknowledgments

As I mentioned at the beginning of the book, this project started as a ten-page "term paper" and evolved over the next two years into a more elaborate endeavor than I anticipated. I learned a great deal along the way and have many people to thank for bringing this memoir to life and into print. Without a push from Professor Howard Stevenson to reflect on what I had learned from my father after his death, I never would have started down this path, but I'm glad he made the suggestion and that I acted on his advice. It has been quite a journey. Some days were painful and emotional, others were filled with laughter. I am ultimately pleased with the result and hope my kids and their kids will be able to appreciate the stories and lessons for years to come.

My uncle, Jay Nichols, was invaluable in helping me fill in the blanks on some of the early stories about Ian when he lived in Kansas. We met in person and talked several times over the phone while writing the memoir. We always ended up chuckling as we reminisced, and he has been a great friend to Ian and me for many years. I am grateful to my "Gruncle" David, Ian's half-brother, who sadly passed away before this book was published. He helped me fine-tune my recollections of Ian's upbringing in Canada and his relationship with Granny. Dad's half-sister, Marie, and I spoke about her delight in finding Ian later in life and the joy they shared as siblings. Bud Scruggs was not only an irreplaceable friend to Dad but also a mentor and true friend to me. I am grateful to him for sharing his wisdom with me in all areas of life. Bud reminded me of Ian's many axioms and business rules, and after reading the early versions of the manuscript contributed invaluable perspective, insight, and feedback. Colby Rollins also read through an initial draft of the book and gave recommendations and edits. He is a valued team member at Cumming Capital Management and knew my father well.

My wife, Kristi, was an early reader of this memoir, and her thoughtful commentary and encouragement gave me the stamina I needed to finish the book. My brother David Cumming, always had my back, encouraged me, and provided love and support that only a brother can. Wayne Fletcher had many great stories about Dad that made us laugh until we cried. Wayne has been like a brother to me and David. He helped look after Ian and spent so much time with Dad and our family; I don't remember when he was not in our lives. I am grateful for his faithful friendship with our family. Natalie Nicholson has unofficially been anointed the family historian. She could excavate every old photo I requested in record time and identify dates and contexts for various events. She was a fantastic help! My stepmother, Annette, answered each of my calls and clarified several dates and events from Ian's life. Heather Stettler supplied constructive and professional editorial advice that added depth to the book. My Chief of Staff, Maria Guarnieri, and Administrative Assistant, Rachel Wentz, keep me going day in and day out. Without them, I don't know where I would be, and this project was no exception!

Kristie Henderson, my "ghost writer," sat with me for many hours, listening to me drone on about my family history. Her empathy, patience, and sincere interest drew information out of me that, in many cases, I had long since forgotten. To say I never would have been able to articulate anything as straightforward as this memoir on my own is an understatement. I hope this book is one of many she crafts in the future.

And finally, to my dad, I love you. Sine Qua Non.

–John D. Cumming

About the Author

John D. Cumming is Co-Chairman of Cumming Capital Management. He also serves as a Board Member and Trustee of the Cumming Foundation. In 1994, John co-founded POWDR Corp., a privately owned company of outdoor lifestyle businesses, and served as the Chief Executive Officer until 2018. He currently serves as Executive Chairman. He also continues to hold many board-level positions, including Chairman of Snowbird Ski & Summer Resort, member of the investment committee of Cumming Trust Management, and Chairman of Crimson Wine Group. John is also a trustee and Chairman Emeritus of the U.S. Ski & Snowboard Foundation and Founder and Chairman Emeritus of The Park City Community Foundation. He lives with his family in Park City, Utah

www.ingramcontent.com/pod-product-compliance
Lightning Source LLC
Chambersburg PA
CBHW051151120626
46547CB00012B/1038